To Sally
& Judi

The Third Floor is a true story of what it was to be a young pregnant teen in the 1960s. Isolated, hidden away, vilified by society, Judi tells her story and thereby the story of many young women like her. It is a story of tragedy and triumph, fear and courage, sadness and joy. But most of all it is a story of overcoming societal ignorance and intolerance, of finding friendships, love, and hope in unlikely places. The Third Floor will make you laugh, cry, and maybe most importantly it will make you think.

Roger B. Graves PH. D.
Licensed Psychologist
Anchorage, Alaska

Our current generation needs to be exposed to this deplorable tale.

Jerry Bakus M.S., M.F.T.

The Third Floor is a story of fear, tragedy and triumph told in the voice of the fifteen-year-old girl who lived it.

THE THIRD FLOOR

Published by Jetstream Publishing
Chico, California
www.jetstreampublishing.com

ISBN: 978-0-615-41771-4

Library of Congress Control Number: 2010916949
Printed in the United States of America

Cover and Interior Design: Connie Ballou, Back Alley Graphics
Copy Editor: Chris Calloway
Cover Photograph: Brittany Morgan
Cover Model: Dana Howes
Miscellaneous Porterville and '60s Photos: Douglas S. McIntosh

DEDICATION

To my daughter Dana and youngest son Spencer, this story is for you and your families. You're part of a plan that was set in motion long before your births. Thank you for your love and respect as we sailed through life with big brother Jeff. I admire you and the rare gifts you've developed: open minds, acceptance of others, and you are both fearless. I am in awe of your choices in life.
Love, Mom

I also want to dedicate this book to all birth mothers who were sent away and forced to relinquish your infants due to social pressures. Step out of the shadows, my friends.

Acknowledgements

Joanie, thank you for saving my letters, and for trusting me with a book about our teenage years. Thanks for years of unconditional friendship and memories.

Tammy, niece and best friend, thank you for typing, helping sort through papers (Bay Breezes), and your efforts to organize me—*Driving Miss Daisy* .

Beth, thanks for being my friend and companion at the Home, for being you and never wavering. You have my highest respect. Thanks for encouraging me and trusting me with our story.

Dana, daughter and business partner, I enjoy your childlike excitement, and thank you for not judging my past. You held down the fort while I wrote my story.

David, thank you for permission to write our story. Thank you for forgiving me and for giving me your love. Thanks for letting me dig through your past and for walking away with the baby book.

Spencer and Cassie, thank you for understanding my choices in life and for all the times we spent on speaker phone correcting chapters; Spencer, you said you ran out of red ink—*funny boy.*

Dr. Mazen Jr., thanks for helping me retrieve my medical records from 1962.

Hairdressers and Clients at Satori Color and Hair Design, you supported my efforts and listened to my rants and raves, offered me ideas and your honest opinions. Thank you.

Nora Profit, my writing instructor and advisor, thank you.

Mike, I appreciate you for stepping up, sending me photos and refreshing my memory. *Romans 8:28.*

Dennis, thank you dear friend for a lifetime of laughs and birthday cards.

My Classmates from Porterville High and Lakeport High, thank you. Your encouragement has played a huge role in long-term healing. The secret is out.

To my husband Peter, a very special thank-you. You encouraged me to get this story out of my head. Thank you for the times you stopped working in your office to help me with computer glitches, answer questions, and print page after page. I appreciate the times you encouraged me to stand up, stretch, and drink a tall glass of water. Love, Judi.

Thanks also to, **Chris Calloway** for copy editing, **Connie Ballou** for cover and interior design, **Brittany Morgan** for cover photography and **Dana Howes,** model for the cover photograph, and Douglas S. McIntosh for allowing me to use your Porterville and 1960s photos.

The
Third Floor

Judi Loren Grace

PROLOGUE

Attitudes and lifestyles changed drastically during the mid 1960s. The first half was a continuation of the fifties, rigid rules and closed minds. There was little communication between a parent and child, and the subject of sex was never discussed. Families took their cue from *Father Knows Best*, and *Ozzie and Harriett*. For a crazy unfettered night, you and your family sang along with Andy Williams. Families gathered around televisions to watch westerns and game shows. Dads enjoyed Friday night boxing. *American Bandstand* was the only window for teens to observe boy-girl interaction.

The mid sixties was the turning point, and it swung away from the core of family values. In 1964 music was transformed. The British invasion happened with the Beatles and the Rolling Stones. The Dave Clark Five and the Kinks hit the airwaves and spun us around. Dusty Springfield sang about her affection for the son of a preacher man and Tom Jones undressed us with his deep, sexy voice.

Music became riskier as the mid sixties progressed. Arlo Guthrie, Jimi Hendrix and Joan Baez sang protests against the Vietnam War. Janis Joplin and the Doors cried out for love. Bob Dylan wailed his nasal saga. We listened. Musically starved teens became drugged with the new sounds and styles. We danced, enjoyed life, and believed the way to live was in the song.

The mid-sixties also brought disappointment and disillusionment. In 1963 John F. Kennedy was assassinated. Unprepared, we faced the senseless killings of Dr. Martin Luther King, Jr. and Bobby Kennedy, both in 1968. Protesters against the war grew in numbers. The war was far worse than anyone expected. Many friends never returned.

The innocent sixties created a metamorphosis before our eyes. 1969 saw Woodstock come alive under a canopy of love and peace. The world watched in shock and awe as free spirits danced and swayed for days in the rain and mud. Haight-Ashbury in San Francisco became the Mecca of lost souls and pseudo-deep thinkers. Sharon Tate begged for her life and Marilyn Monroe took hers.

In the early part of the sixties, girls endured peer pressure and a double standard. If you didn't go "all the way" with a boy you were labeled a tease or frigid. If you did give in and didn't get pregnant you were lucky. If you did become pregnant, you were damned and ostracized.

My story begins in the summer of '62. A school-girl crush with Tom and the heartfelt confrontation with my parents led me to Booth Memorial Home and Hospital. I will share with you the daily workings of a home filled to capacity with girls who were cast out of society, the daily routine inside a home for unwed mothers, the lack of compassion and information, the military style rules, the medical procedures, none of which our parents imagined.

Girls clung to youthful hopes, with innocent fears of the unknown. Strangers bonded together by insecurity fed relationships to last a lifetime. We are the girls who disappeared and, in a flurry of lies and denial, reappeared. This is the story of an unnoticed minority who weathered change and came back to claim their losses.

My story first began to seep onto paper 23 years prior to publication. This process of remembering and reliving my summer in a home was more difficult than I had anticipated. I stopped. I tackled it again in 1996 and failed again.

Finally in 2009 I began again with the help of a client, Marycarol. She is an adoptee and she coached me as I typed my story. Another client, Chris, took me to a writers' meeting. Together we listened and soon I joined a writing class. My words began to flow with the help from my instructor, Nora. Together we hammered out my story which took all winter and into the following summer.

I contacted my girlfriend Joanie and she mailed the letters I had sent her during my stay at the Home. I quietly read the letters she had saved and was shocked at my maturity level, which was very young. I wrote about my fears and loneliness.

I contacted my physician and he sent away for my medical records. The information from medical posts from attending or visiting nurses and doctors was valuable, and confirmed my suspicions of weight loss.

My clients Marycarol, Chris, Sherry and Sandy were my strength. My daughter was my shadow and kept a close eye on her obsessive mom.

This is a journey of lost innocence, embarrassment, hope and ultimately the realization that a veil of shame has been lightly draped over my being, and has been there for most of my life. I hope to reach birth mothers in such a way they will feel comfortable enough to step out of their shame and live life in transparency. Enjoy who you are and accept the past. It could have happened to anyone.

I lived in the home for unwed mothers on Garden Street for 98 days.

I was told I was five months pregnant on a Monday.

My parents drove me to Oakland on a Monday.

I delivered my baby on a Monday.

PART ONE

YOUNG JUDI

Most people confuse my height with maturity, but I'm a kid on stilts. Anyone can mimic a grown up girl with short skirts and big hair. I am fifteen. Thirteen is closer to my maturity level. I don't even know how to boil an egg. Father is sending me away to save the family name. I will grow larger, deliver my baby, return as if nothing has changed, and no one will be the wiser.

I remember being rocked as a baby in my mother's arms. I remember age three, taking a bubble bath. My happiest memory is as a four-year-old. I am wearing a soft cotton dress, light yellow. I am running as fast as the wind across the school yard. My dress soars around me as the wind whips against my face. I love being free.

I love my family; my cousins, aunts, uncles, grandparents, and the house that shelters me; our small town and the pastor at our church. I am happy and have no fears except snakes. My mother was raised in Arkansas and tells snake stories. I love to sing and wait on the front porch for my daddy to come home from work.

I've managed to mature faster than most girls my age. I've grown tall and appear older. My body and my brain are out of sync. I like boys and I'm curious. I wonder about marriage, the love between a man and a woman. I watch my aunts and uncles, the way they kiss each other on their wedding day. I decide that God also watches this marriage. On a day full of fluffy clouds God drops a seed, and that's how I get a cousin. I'm eleven years old when I decide it is a simple seed drop.

When I'm twelve my sister sits me down at the kitchen table one afternoon and tells me the truth, the real story of conception. My mother stands silent with her back to us squishing hamburger and eggs together, the makings of a meatloaf, as I learn the truth. I am mortified and spin into accelerated imagery. It is this accelerated imagery that lands me where I am today.

PORTERVILLE

My hometown of Porterville is nestled in the
foothills east of the San Joaquin Valley almost
exactly between Fresno and Bakersfield, about
65 miles east or west in either direction,
against the foothills. Our main farming crops
are oranges, lemons, and avocados. In the
spring the valley is engulfed in the sweet
scent of orange blossoms. Warmth from the
spring sun and blue skies captures a safe and
idyllic place to be raised. Kids run free up and
down their block, play with friends, ride
bikes, or spend the day on empty school grounds.
On weekends, sometimes we go to the city
plunge with friends, who are friends for
life. Sometimes we head south of town to
the roller rink and spin around for awhile.
Most of our parents went to high school
together and most dads are WWII veterans.

Winters are late. Fall is the longest season, windy with beautiful fall colors. Thanksgiving always has perfect weather. One time in January it snowed; we had about two inches. It covered our town with a thin blanket of white. I was a sophomore and school was out for the day. Most of us returned home. My mother and I pushed the Priscilla curtains to the side and looked out the bay window to stare at the winter wonderland.

When I grew up in the 1950s, Porterville was only fourteen square miles with approximately 10,000 people. Known for agriculture, besides the groves of citrus there is a variety of dairy farms and cattle ranches. As crazy as is seems, I love the smell of freshly baled hay and distant dairy farms mixed with citrus. It's the smell of home and anyone born and raised in the valley knows this smell.

Our high school band has girls who walk in front of the band and spell out the name of our town; they're called the Orange Blossoms. I tried out to be an Orange Blossom my freshman year, but my legs were too skinny and my hair too short. I am still envious when I watch a parade.

The first weekend in April is the Springville Rodeo. Even though I know nothing about horses or ranching, it's a big deal to dress western style and watch the events. The only horse I have ever sat on was Trigger. In the early 1950s my parents took us girls to Roy Rogers' ranch and Roy and a ranch hand lifted me up and sat me on his famous horse. Trigger stepped back, twitched his tail, and I slid off the back.

In school I established lifelong friendships as most people do in small towns. This is a bonus because our family moves every other year, then back again, so I'm in some class pictures and not in others. My dad, the Deputy Agricultural Commissioner, was transferred to Exeter, a small town 30 miles northeast, then he would get another promotion and back we'd go to Porterville.

I was growing taller every day, leaving my short mother in my shadow. My legs are longer than anyone's I've seen. My grandmother likes to rub my legs up and down with her gentle hands. She and my mother talk about my long legs, while I lie there listening to them talk over me, enjoying my grandmother's soft touch.

There is nothing to do on weekends except drag Main. My friends always drive my car because I only have a learner's permit. We drive down Main Street, then down Olive Street, make a U turn at Coleman's fast foods and drive back, same streets, U turn and back again. With our windows down, cars pass by with hands waving, honks, and yelling to come over. Guys stand around at a closed gas station leaning on their cars; sometimes a wave, or a wave down to turn into the parking lot. Gwen in her parents' green car she named Super Pickle, me with my Opel full of girls, Rita and Dennis in Burger's red Nova, Murray and Andrea in her pink and gray '55 Chevy, Norman in his father's '54 maroon Coup de Ville.

We drive down Olive Street and back down to Main, to Snow White drive-in, turn at Gang Sue's Chinese restaurant and head back toward Coleman's. This continual cruising back and forth is approximately one mile in each direction. We must have put fifty miles a night on our odometers, and gas has spiked up to 29 cents a gallon. Sometimes we'd go to the Porter Theater and watch a good movie like *West Side Story*, *To Kill a Mockingbird*, or *Summer Place* where Sandra Dee loses her virginity to Troy Donahue in the bath house on the boat dock. Some of our friends work behind the counter and we get free popcorn.

Our group gets ready together. Usually we meet at Joanie's house because her older sister Janet has some really cute Lanz dresses. Sometimes we wear tight jeans and tight blouses. Getting our hair nice and big, clothes fly through the air and the Four Seasons sing in the background. We wait for a honk or jump into my Opel and off we go, maybe to a high school dance.

Many summer nights are spent with another set of friends playing cards. The kitchen table of big time card sharks consists of; Rita, Murray, Dennis, Norman, Andrea and me. We play Pit, a game of collecting matching commodities such as: corn, oats, rice, flax, barley, and wheat. When the bell rings everyone yells their trade. It's insanity as the room erupts with loud voices and trades. I begin to laugh because Rita yells so loud she seems angry, "corn, three corn, corn, corn three corn" I become weak with laughter as she stretches across the table and takes whatever cards she needs and shoves three mystery cards back into my limp hand. Murray also joins in and helps herself. Through tears of laughter I can only whisper, "oats, oats, two oats" The bell rings and the dealer yells "Pit," game over. We consume sodas and play well into the night.

Our hometown is a safe haven. My "situation" the summer of '62 shocked us into reality. Even though it was a secret, word got around. I have changed. I try to be the same funny girl, but I feel a dark cloud over me most of the time. If everyone starts to get loud and act silly, I feel myself retreat far away in thought. I feel out of step with my friends and some of the jokes and drinking seem immature. I pretend to have a good time. I only feel safe if I am with one of my friends on a one on one. I hate being herded, and never again do I feel at ease in a group.

No Information—Only suggestions

Mother never mentions sex. This subject is taboo. In our household there is never a discussion about the future, babies, where they come from, or relationships. No words of warning. Mother only talks to me about my wedding day I will have someday, and the big white dress I will wear.

One Saturday, out of the blue, Mother gets the courage to talk to me about something very important; she mentions maturing. I'm thirteen and ready for this talk. Mother suggests we go into her bedroom; I follow along like a duckling in a pond full of anticipation. We head to her room and I eagerly step into my window of adulthood. Mother begins to tell me that if my breasts ever begin to hurt, to never rub them; if I do, they will grow. I listen and blink as she goes on to say that they will grow and be big like hers. She unbuttons her blouse and lets it fall to one side, then she slides her bra strap off of her shoulder to reveal the evidence: deep red gouges on top of her shoulders made by the weight of her bra straps that cradle her monster boulders. I look closely, touch the indentation with my finger and see the redness, feel sorry for my mother and realize her story is true, and not a pretty sight.

Since that day, I've remembered our mother-daughter talk many times. One reason I remember this so vividly is because it is the only talk we ever had about becoming a woman. In the future my breasts did swell and feel sore, especially before my period, but I always restrained from a relief rub. The one big mistake I made was telling my girlfriends. Rita and Murray keep a watchful eye on my development and Murray often mentions that she's noticed I haven't been rubbing my boobs; then Rita and Murray toss their heads back and laugh like idiots. All three of us are as flat as pancakes. But I have to wonder why my mother's were so huge.

For some reason Mother's responsibilities in raising girls did not go beyond shopping, cooking, laundry and cleaning, and touching our breasts. It's Mother Nature who will teach us. I spoke with my girlfriend Mary and she told me that she was in her bedroom and began to bleed. She had no idea what menstruation meant. Mary said she walked into the kitchen, interrupted her mother who was cooking dinner and began to cry. Her mother asked her what was wrong and Mary, through her sobs, replied, "I'm dying."

When it was my turn and I started my monthly curse, I was not quite twelve. I was at home; mother was at the grocery store. I went to the bathroom and there it was. I had to stop the flow and I knew not to use anything nice of Mother's. I did the only logical thing a girl could do. I leaped up, ran down the hall to my sister's bedroom, opened up the heavy lid to her hope chest, put a towel between my legs, and quickly returned to the living room and continued to watch cartoons.

I heard Mother coming through the back door and listened to her as she put the groceries away. I continued to watch *Casper the Friendly Ghost*. I didn't mention anything because it didn't matter, and I wanted to see the ending. My sister came home, dropped her books and walked into the living room. She sat down next to me on the couch and noticed her prize towel sticking out from my pedal pushers. She asked me why I was sitting on her special towel and I told her I had to because of the blood. Bobbie screamed like I had just stuck her with a knife, mother ran into the living room to see what had happened and in an instant our home was pandemonium. Mother showed me where the pads are kept under the sink, and showed me the elastic belt and the weird little metal thing to intertwine the floppy end of the pad. While my class about sanitary napkins was going on, my sister was washing her towel in the washing machine and yelling about stains, new towels, and marriage. She was stomping around like I had just ruined her wedding and she wasn't even dating.

One day at school Andrea told me she heard Dennis and Norman say the word clitoris. She liked this word. The following week she went to her aunt's baby shower. Andrea said to a room full of ladies, "If I ever have a baby girl I want to name her Clitoris." The room fell silent, her aunt stared in disbelief and her mother turned her back and began to do the dishes. I guess she picked the wrong name.

Another friend told me that her mother told her to never do anything wrong. She thought about this statement and was bewildered. Her mother gave her no boundaries and no gauge. Her mother smokes, drinks, is divorced and plays cards. She said she had to wonder what "wrong" was, and if her mother was right or wrong. There was never an explanation. Simply do what is right, not wrong. If her mother is having a highball with a cigarette, she surmises this is right. We went over this and I knew better. My mother only read the *Bible* and cooked healthy foods. I knew not to smoke. I did know how to play cards, and I have had a velvet hammer (grape sloe gin and orange juice). It was illegal but not wrong, and I knew not to tell.

Naturally when I was blooming with pregnancy and unaware of my condition, my breasts were filling out and sore. For relief I wanted to wrap my upper body in a hot towel and curl up. I never did. I never touched them and they continued to grow. *Mother was wrong.*

CONCEPTION

Tom has chased me around since early summer. He is relentless in his pursuit and he's heavily armed with charm. This night is different. I have the distinct feeling Tom is getting bored or anxious with me. I am not dreamy-eyed in love, but I am in awe of him—his vintage car, his reputation, and sitting next to him makes me popular by association. He had been his senior class president.

We drive around town until we hear about a party at Lloyd's house south of town. We go there to socialize, and he always brings me a beer. I hate the taste, but it makes me appear older. We talk to friends, listen to music, sit on the couch and pretend to be having fun. Later on I am to meet up with my best girlfriends so we can talk about what we did and where we ended up on this cold foggy night. Joanie is a dark-haired, green-eyed beauty, and Trudy a short, peppy blue-eyed bombshell.

My parents are in San Jose visiting my aunt and uncle for the holidays. My sister's in charge of watching over me, even though she's moved out and rents a room from her friend Pat. This is the same as asking a movie star to stay home and darn socks during the Oscars. She's an absentee sitter. I knew she would be so I planned a slumber party.

My date with Tom is no different than all the others. It ends in a debate over sex, me thinking up excuses and Tom explaining them all away. But this night, I give in. I sort of give in. There is no way out. He's buffaloed me and I have no recourse. It isn't painful, and I am not sure if we actually did anything or not. I want to keep him happy and interested in me, and I have no idea why. We share no passion and I'm fearful of too much nuzzling up to him; he'll get mixed messages. My girlfriends cheer me on and think he is great and I'm a very lucky girl. He's cute and popular, but it's not worth it. He is a brat. I didn't comprehend I could've said no as he continued to wear me down.

It's late. He drops me off at my house and he doesn't walk me to the front door. I jump out of the car and run up the walkway to the front porch, turn and look back to wave goodbye, but he is gone, engulfed in the fog like a phantom date.

I tiptoe down the hall toward my bedroom just in time to see Trudy doing a header through my bedroom window. She drops in arms first. I guess she thought the door was locked because it sticks. I stand with my hands on my hips like a mother. She says she thought the door was locked—no, it sticks—and we laugh like crazy. We undress and scrounge for quilts. There are already girls sleeping on the floor.

I see headlights as Joanie and Bill pull up to the curb. Joanie runs in ten minutes later through the back door. I look at Trudy. Joanie undresses quickly and we dive in and cuddle under the cold sheets and layers of quilts. We steal each other's body heat. Three pals in bed all giddy and happy is a moment to cherish. Our home is filled with Christmas decorations, the scent of pine fills the house, and I'm cozy and sleepy between my two best friends.

Trudy starts talking about her night. She was up at a ranch party with loud music, but she said it was chilly and not as much fun as she pretended. The ranch is higher than the blanket of fog covering our town. The drive down the mountain road is dangerous, like dropping into a glass of milk. Trudy saw Betty at the party but didn't invite her to stay over; Betty is too wild for our blood. Now that we know we're all in safe for tonight, we nestle in.

Trudy asks Joanie where she and Bill were tonight. Joanie says they were dragging Main, but it was too foggy. She says they passed us, recognized Tom's car, heading south. I chime in and say we were heading to Lloyd's house for a party. Joanie says they decided to go to a musical at the high school. This is Joanie's first date with Trudy's brother Bill.

It is not only a foggy night, I am in a fog as well. I have a confession; I'll wait for the right time. Every Sunday morning Joanie and I have a ritual. We drive to Murray Park, park by the duck pond under the same palm tree, and sip sodas. We tell each other secrets of the weekend and share stories about life and ideas. We explore thoughts about boys and relationships. Our conversations are innocent and shallow. We have no material to draw from.

Trudy asks me about my relationship with Tom. Yes, of course we were together; he's been chasing me all summer and fall, and now it's almost the New Year. She asks what we did, where we went, who we saw. Joanie is whispering, maybe talking to herself or to the moon. She's still consumed with the dangers of the dense fog and how scary it was to drive to my house. Joanie goes on to say the fog was so thick you couldn't see your hand if you held it outstretched.

The other girls remain asleep on my bedroom carpet. Trudy and I continue to talk. I whisper that I was not only with him, but this night was different and things seemed to get out of hand. I tell her about running out of excuses, which resulted in you-know-what. "He keeps badgering me and he makes me feel stupid," I continue. "He accused me of keeping myself from him. Then he actually got angry with me. I went too far; I mean, really far." Joanie is still and quiet. Trudy scoots closer and in a whisper she asks if I am still a virgin and I whisper back, "I think so." I couldn't answer this question with honesty.

It only took minutes this night to decide my future.

I am two hours into my pregnancy.

Next morning when we get up everyone's hair looks like an explosion. Five of us meet in the kitchen in mismatched clothes, pour milk on Rice Krispies, and quickly return to my bedroom to put our feet under blankets and eat. Connie has to get her parents' car home; she leaves early. One by one the girls return home: Joyce, Trudy, Neva and Joanie.

New Year's Eve is next week. Joanie and I decide this special night will be for just the two of us. We have our cokes and peanuts in place. Her mom makes snacks and brings in a hi-fi. She puts on Johnny Mathis and leaves. We practice makeup, especially eyeliner. We polish her sister's copper belt. We snack, giggle and gossip. We agree to nix Johnny and turn on the radio instead. We listen to Wolfman Jack out of L.A. and his lonesome wolf cry. Now with some great music, we share dance moves.

She tells me about a new invention her sister found. It's like a tiny white cotton cigar. You use this instead of a Kotex pad, and it's called a Pursette. It's smaller than a regular Tampax, with a string attached. It's supposed to go up inside of you, but not very far. This will stop the flow. Joanie says we can swim and play in P.E. and do lots of things. She shows me some of these from her big sister's stash in her top drawer. We take turns in the bathroom, trying them out. It's more like a science project. We hate them; it's painful. Mine is dry, and I think it will never come back out. I pull on the string and call through the door in panic for instructions. Joanie yells back from the other side of the door. She tells me to put my leg on the side of the sink and pull really hard. I yell that my guts are coming out. We fall against the door laughing, one outside, one in. Once I get this torture thing out of me we fall over on her bed. Ouch ... We agree we are both stupid and to never try that again. Move on, it's inching toward midnight.

We don't have much time to make New Year's resolutions. Someone keeps driving by her house and honking. That someone is Bill. We peek out the front window between the drapes, but don't respond. I know he likes her and she is thrilled. Truth is, he is consumed with her, and so am I. A tug of war over Joanie begins. He finally leaves us alone and we have time to think and write our New Year's resolutions. Hers: "I am going to focus on my homework and prepare for college and grow my hair."

Mine: "I will turn over a new leaf, be a better student. 1962 is about new beginnings. I'll grow my hair too."

At the stroke of midnight we clank our Coke bottles and guzzle, eat Cheeze Whiz on crackers. Then the good part. We have saved the best for last—a box of Cracker Jacks.

"Here's to the coming new year of promise. Goodbye 1961."

Five days into my pregnancy.

CONFIRMATION

The second week in April the bleeding starts again, a heavy crimson flow that continues for days. Each day I get up and dress for school, eat breakfast, throw up, brush my teeth, and walk one block to Rita's house and wait for Murray to drive around the corner on two wheels in her hot Chevy. Off we go to school. Rita and Murray are on the school tennis team. I'm on the swim team. After school, I take the school bus to the swimming pool at the park, practice, and ride back to the high school where Rita and Murray wait for me. We jump into Murray's Chevy and off we'd go to Rita's, then I walk home.

I miss a few meets and swim lessons because of my unannounced menstrual cycle. When able, I practice for two hours, swimming in 52° water with my ankles tied together, dragging a large empty tomato juice can as a weight, and pulling myself with my arms, or do laps for an hour, or sometimes swim laps with my wrists tied together and kicking only.

When I was eleven years old, I won the gold cup and also second place for the Junior Olympics in the California relay races. My position was anchor. Swimming competitively was exhilarating and fulfilling at the same time. Now I'm on the high school swim team, I swim with a guy named Scott. He is handsome, and I spotted him the first day of school my freshman year. What luck we were on the same swim team. He is a friend and someone I can trust if I miss my ride. Having him on the same team makes the rough practices easier, especially when he wears his nylon racing trunks. My life is school, swim team, homework, girl talk on the phone, and partying on weekends.

One morning my mother tells me that after school I need to come straight home because she has made a doctor's appointment for me. I wondered if she and my grandma got their heads together and decided I might be pregnant. I've been sick a lot, put on some weight and my boobs have filled out—finally they fill a bra. Maybe I've been living in denial all these months, and my mother is savvy to pregnancy and the symptoms. It is out of character for my shy, passive mother to take charge of anything. I wonder if she suspects something. But I'm not pregnant; you don't bleed when you're pregnant. I drive us to the doctor with my learners permit. The doctor is not my usual doctor. This doctor is female, a doctor who only sees women about female stuff.

Today at school I don't mention my doctor's appointment. It doesn't seem abnormal for a girl to get her cycle straightened out. My mother is playing her cards close to her chest. We don't talk all the way to the doctor's office. I am oblivious and not worried. I'm just eating poorly and swimming too hard.

When the nurse calls my name I stand up and go in. I take off my clothes as instructed and put on a little cloth dress with an open back. I sit on the edge of the examining table, my long skinny legs swinging back and forth with no thoughts in my head. The nurse takes my blood pressure and temperature. The doctor comes in. She is tall, thin, with angular features and long, gray, fuzzy hair pulled back into a messy bun. She orders me to lie down and scoot down toward the edge. She is cold, blunt and gruff, with the bedside manner of a snapping turtle and no small talk. She doesn't know me, but she is treating me like a convict.

My biggest concern is her seeing my privates. This is my first exam and it is not a good experience. Plus, a woman touching a woman, come on. Give me a break! Embarrassed, I close my eyes and think only good thoughts. I think about swimming laps and doing my curl turn, faster and faster. I slide my bottom to the end as instructed and then the doctor tells me to relax my legs and let them fall open. She has a glove on; this is the moment of truth. I am getting examined down there.

She doesn't ask me one question about my cycle. She puts her finger inside me, pushs around, puts her other hand on my stomach and pushs down and around. As she pulls off her rubber glove, she walks away, tosses it in the trash, and at the exact moment says, "You are five months pregnant, but you obviously know that." I am just stunned, shocked. What about the blood, my periods? You can't have periods and be pregnant. I feel alone and scared. The doctor seems to be very annoyed with me. I feel trapped.

I haven't been with Tom since December 26th, and this is mid-April. I don't know if I secretly knew and thought it would just go away if I kept up my usual routines, but the throwing up, the pickle craving, my breasts growing; I'm speechless. The entire exam lasted ten minutes and I didn't ask her one question. She jots something on a piece of paper and walks out. Ashen faced, I dress and go to my mother. She stands and we head to the car, get in and drive home in silence.

I go to my room, lie down and begin to cry, first sobbing and then wailing. My mother lies down beside me and asks me what is wrong. She knows; she needs confirmation like me. I tell her I am pregnant. She sits up next to me and begins to cry. She asks me how far along I am and I tell her, five months. She walks away, and I see her face, tears streaming down her cheeks. She is grieving for me. I have no idea where she goes or what she does. I just lie there in a ball crying, too upset to phone Joanie.

I lie in bed with tears streaming down my face and think; in January I missed my period, and I called Tom and told him I might be pregnant. He said he needed to talk to his friend Arnie who can help. I waited until February then began to spot. This soon turned into a massive flow. A sigh of relief. I never heard from Tom again or his hatched plan with Arnie. I chalked it up to a bad judgment call on my part and never looked back, not until this dark April day.

TELLING MY FAMILY

Telling my mother I'm pregnant was horrible, but not as bad as the next confrontation: my dad. Mom and I cried together. Then I hear her on the phone, and I just lie there and wait for my bedroom door to open and engulf me in the flames of hell. My father will soon be on his way home. Mother loves me but she is never able to express it. There is no hugging and very little touching. Her love is simply known with that sweet mother love I feel. Because of a small stroke she suffered when I was three, her ability to express herself was damaged. Mother caters to us and waits on us as if she is a maid.

I lie there on my bed stunned, scared and humiliated. I wait there for the rest of the afternoon with my radio playing. The songs that once made me think and enjoy are now noisy background sounds. It seems an eternity, but it is only an hour until I hear my sister drive up; the car door slams, and then running footsteps. She is fast, but not as fast as my two long legs as I sprint down the hall and lock myself in the bathroom. Hiding in there I wait, leaning up against the counter. I am in the only safe place to hide. I can't face my sister. She bangs her fist on the door and begs me to let her in. She is yelling through the door how sorry she is and I listen and she cries.

Bobbie is six years older than me. She encouraged the relationship I had with this guy. I have to blame someone, so I guess I could start with my sister. He is popular and out of high school, an older guy. It never occurred to me that he isn't going anywhere in life. I remember her telling me how lucky I am to be with such a popular guy. But I have to admit, even if she had warned me, I probably wouldn't have listened.

Bobbie is still in the hallway, pleading for me to unlock the door. She is clearly upset and sorry; she sounds frantic. I tell her to please go away. She seems much more upset than me; her reaction startles me. I ask her to please go away again and again, but she isn't having any part of my plea.

More than an hour passes when she hears a click. I tell her I am coming out and to stand back. She rushes in; mother is still crying in the hallway. I back up to the sink and listen to her jabber on and on about a plan to help me. Our father is coming home from work and we both know this is going to be a huge ugly scene. My father has an explosive temper and I am clearly in deep trouble. I need to get back to my room and rest. I ask Bobbie again to please calm down and let me rest. Dad is coming home. She finally realizes what is going to happen. She tells me not to worry and says she loves me, and then does a disappearing act. Waiting for my father to come home from work is a tortuous couple of hours. With Bobbie gone I rest and prepare, trying to cope with this nightmare.

My father is running for mayor; he's assembled a Dixieland band with huge banner that reads: vote for good 'ol Charlie. He dresses for our centennial celebration in a black top hat, pin striped slacks, tails and spats; he walks in front of his band and hands out cigars and cards during events or parades. He will be angry and mortified. He just won the beard contest; he is up to his neck in campaign tactics.

My bedroom door is closed. I lie on my back in silence and wait. I am sure he knows by now. Waiting for my father to enter our house is like waiting at the gallows; the floor should drop under me any second. I am embarrassed and scared and confused, still too numb with fear to call Joanie. I hear the words from the doctor, "You are five months pregnant and you obviously know that," still ringing in my head. It is April at the end of my sophomore year. Life is good, or so I thought. I have had periods; this doesn't add up. I bled like a stuck hog in February. My mother took me to a doctor because of my erratic bleeding, missed periods and spotting. I am filling out and loving the curves. My mother has huge breasts, and I thought I was following in her footsteps.

I hear my father's car, the sound of his footsteps. Mother gently opens my door and says in a soft voice, "Judi, honey, your father wants to talk to you." I hear the words I have been dreading all day long; the deep voice of my father saying, "Judi, you need to come to the living room."

I walk down the narrow hallway to the living room. Frozen in my emotions, frightened and numb, I put one foot in front of the other, trembling. I can do this. He is sitting in his wide, square, brown tweed chair facing the screen door. The sun is setting, the sky is pink and the living room is aglow. Gently I sit down opposite of him. I raise my head to make eye contact. He is handsome, tall and thin. His brown hair sparkles with gray at the temples. He sits staring out the screen door. With the sunset on his face I notice his crystal blue eyes are full of tears. He cries for me.

He looks at me with his glistening wet eyes and asks me one question, "Who is the father?"

I tell him. He gazes out the door again and doesn't look back at me.

My sister Bobbie is back with her daughter. Mother and Bobbie are in the kitchen. She waits for me to get in trouble, listens. She is worried and quiet as they prepare dinner. Bobbie always argues with our parents and never learned to listen. She's had many harsh spankings from Father, but never from our mother. I was the one who listened and minded. I learned from watching her, what not to do. But I don't get into trouble tonight. It was worse. I broke his heart. It broke my heart to see him cry for the first time.

CONFRONTATION

Two days after my pregnancy is confirmed, I sit in my room hiding from would-be gossip hounds, dealing with the news as I forge ahead. I finally tell the three friends I know will understand and not judge me and help. Joanie is in a position to ward off any snippets of bad rumors, and my friends Dennis and Trudy can help squelch the fire. The sun comes up as usual; mother cooks scrambled eggs and toast. I drink a glass of milk, brush my teeth, walk to Rita's and wait for Murray to drive us to school. I don't mention my condition. We have a different type of relationship, more on the innocent spectrum and childlike teasing.

I'm ready for the next step of my journey. I haven't missed any school and have kept up with homework. I'm tired at the end of the day and the swim coach seems more hell-bent on insane practices. Some things never change; I swim with 32-ounce empty tomato cans strapped to my ankles and pull with my arms as I swim laps until she blows her whistle. Then we take off the cans, strap our wrists together and dive in. We obediently kick our legs until we are dead.

After school I wait for my sister Bobbie. She promises me she has a plan. She has all the answers. My sister is newly divorced, her daughter Tammy is a welcome family blessing, my pregnancy is not.

Bobbie pulls up to our house. She'll solve my problem. I knew she would think of something; she always does. I feel relief seeing her and I'm ready to try anything. She and her friend Pat have a plan to end my pregnancy, and this is how it's going to unfold. She reminds me that they both work at the State Mental Hospital and to sit tight. Their plan is to get medication from another worker; this might take a day or two. They know how to abort pregnancies. This crazy notion is my only hope.

While my sister tries to get this mysterious medication to terminate my pregnancy, I'm at school. It doesn't occur to me that to terminate a pregnancy at five months could kill me, that I could bleed to death. I have known about my pregnancy for forty-eight hours and the clock continues to tick.

The one and only thing that matters is my reputation. My dad's lost respect for me, and of course, his campaign to win the election for mayor. Naive to the dangers, I trust my sister and her sidekick Pat. I've no idea what's inside of me at five months; I just have a little bump.

Tom is supposed to be here this evening to confront my father. He's a no-show. This is a huge error in judgment; no one dismisses my father. I climb into bed and curl up to sleep after a long day.

My father's plan is to have his friend fly us to Las Vegas for a quickie wedding. I utter, "Okay Daddy," but the thought of marrying Tom is absurd. The idea almost makes me laugh. I really don't know him that well, just a guy around town. He happens to live down the street, he noticed me and he's been pursuing me for a year. He's blessed with the gift of gab. He's very clever and won't take no for an answer. I'm in a panic and need to phone Joanie. She will die when I tell her the details of the last few days.

I hear a faint knock at the door. I look toward my clock radio; it's 9:00 P.M. He did show up after all, and he is so late. My father is a stickler for promptness. I have to smile because of rule number one: no one keeps my father waiting. I listen for conversation. I hear my dad's voice. He's angry, aggressive and his voice is stern and directed at someone. I am sure he grits his teeth, which is always a bad sign. I hear another voice too. Yes, there are more than two people out there. I forgot to tell my father that I have taken a stance against marriage, and now I am too chicken to tell him. It only seems like yesterday I learned about the birds and the bees.

The only movie I saw about life's cycles and changes was in fifth grade. I skipped home and never gave it another thought. I did remember the movie's byline: "If you have cramps, always fix your hair and put on a nice dress." In 1962 there is no information on sex, pregnancy, or stages of the fetus. There are two options: homes for unwed mothers and shotgun weddings. Our family is ripped apart. The cool night breeze smells of orange blossoms; it doesn't fit. I skip dinner, secluding myself in my room and curl up into a ball. I wait for my sister to help me end this nightmare. Better to starve than to face my family.

It's D-day.

My father calls me into the living room to face Tom. I hop up, rip the rollers out of my hair and tousle it with my fingers, smear Vaseline on my lips. I want to look good when I watch my father in action. He's Perry Mason if he wants to be. I walk down the hall when I realize I'm wearing my mother's pink floral nightgown. She's 4'11" and I'm 5'9". Minds are a powerful thing; this coming scene is crystal clear. It's etched into my mind as if burned with acid. I step into the living room in slow motion, sit down on our brown tweed couch positioned next to the hallway door and wall heater. Directly behind the couch is a large picture of Jesus praying on the Mount. I drop to the couch before I faint, tug on the hem of my mother's nightgown but it's no use. I can feel the night air on my bare legs.

There sit three males; my father takes a seat at the opposite end of the couch. Tom sits in my father's favorite chair, and there sits Mike in our maple dining chair. I wait and wonder what this is all about. It is much too private for Tom to bring a friend. Mike's face is red. I'm sure mine is either pink from embarrassment or white from lack of blood flow. Mike has a look across his face that people have when they are strapped on a ride at the fair, just before they lose it. Tom keeps his head down and never looks up. I hope Mike doesn't pass out and fall backward. I see Tom for what he is.

My father looks toward me with his piercing blue eyes, but this time I see the look of a man who is about to pounce. My heart beats out of my chest. The next scene is more shocking than I ever dreamed, and I have a vivid imagination.

My father looks at me and says, "Judi, both these boys say that either one of them could be the father of your child. Is this true?" My heart pounds so loud I can't hear. I'm having an out-of-body experience. I hear the question seconds before the thumping begins. The room starts to spin. Some part of my brain comes to my rescue. I quickly regain my composure, look toward my father, look him straight in the eye and in a clear and direct voice answer with one word, "No."

"Then go to your room," he replies. I run down the hall and jump into bed and pull the sheets up to my chin.

Then I hear his speech. "Judi is only fifteen years old. Mike, you are nineteen and Tom, you are twenty. I will have both of you sons of bitches thrown in jail for statutory rape."

Mike responds quickly with, "Sir, I joined the Navy and I leave on Tuesday."

My father shoots back with, "Mike, I was a Navy man for nine years. I will notify the Navy and you will be tossed into the brig for a very long time." No sounds from Tom.

I wish Joanie was here. She will die.

My dad continues, "I will go after both of you with everything I have, and Tom, I will hang you out to dry, make no mistake about that." They both say they understand and the front door closes. I'm ice cold, betrayed and I feel like a whore. I've just been stabbed in the back and my father slapped in the face. I lie in bed numb until sleep finally brings peace. I am awakened by the sound of another knock at the door. I look at my clock radio and it's 1:45 A.M. My father gets out of bed, steps outside to the front porch. He is outside for fifteen minutes and comes back in, softly shuts the door and goes back to bed.

The next morning my father comes into my bedroom and tells me about the late night visitor. I listen with both ears. It was Mike, returning to tell my father that he was helping his friend out of a jam but he couldn't go through with it. He said earlier in the day he got a phone call from Tom saying, "Judi is pregnant. I need your help."

He asked Mike to tell my dad that he might be the father too. If Mike did this he wouldn't get into any trouble. It's a boys' club code blue, or perhaps an Indian myth. Mike is a good friend to everyone and he agreed to do this for Tom. What he discovered that night was that he has a good heart and a conscience.

Mike said that he sat down the street in his car for about two hours thinking he could help the situation by marrying me. I would have agreed to that, and I could keep my baby. I don't know if I can ever fully excuse his behavior and accept his apology. I'll recover, but Mike can never take away the crushing pain this caused my father.

PREGNANCY SOLUTIONS

Nurse Bobbie shows up two days later with "meds." Time is of the essence. Bobbie's only thoughts are to help me terminate. The only thought we have in our little pea-brains is to abort and save me from an arranged marriage. I realize I'm entering my fifth month, and this may only make things more difficult. Naturally she boosts the dosage. Bobbie busies herself with her simple plan; Mother sits at the kitchen table reading her Bible. My sister phones Pat for directions and consultation. She is on a mission.

My mother and grandmother have a hotline between them and I can feel my ears burning. Also in this triangle of gossip is my mother's sister Doris. The three of them solve most of the world's problems. I am hot news in our family and it is heating up the wires from my mother to her mother and her sister, and then to all of my mother's brothers, all six of them and their wives, then my cousins. I am not sure if the news of the abortion clinic in our kitchen makes it to the hot wires, but my condition is big news within our tight family circle. I assume this anyway; maybe I'm getting paranoid. I know I am nervous.

Bobbie tells me this mixture will make me sick to my stomach and also give me cramps, but it is part of the process. I guess she is in the business of aborting babies as she begins to toss out scenarios. Although she has never done anything like this before, she acts like she is a doctor. Bobbie asks Mom to help us. Mother closes her Bible and walks over.

Mother takes a long wooden spoon and begins to stir the castor oil with the orange juice as Bobbie instructs. After stirring she is unable to get a blend. She gives up, hands the oily spoon to my sister and lets her stir for a while. The oil will not blend with the orange juice and it continues to separate and bubble to the top. Slowly she mixes and asks for Mom's help; the spoon goes back and forth.

Bobbie tells me to gulp it down quickly and not think about the oil bubbles that pop to the surface. I look down on this greasy moving drink, dark orange on the bottom and lighter orange with oil on the top. The oil is not only cresting at the top, it separates, then boom, a bubble shoots out the top.

My mother lets my sister hand this huge glass of poison to me, then Mother excuses herself from participating. Bobbie tells me to drink it and hands me some white pills. This life saver turns out to be a combination of quinine tablets and castor oil, a sure-fire way to end a pregnancy. I have no idea what these pills might do, but since Bobbie is sort of a doctor, she says to do it and so I do.

She says I should have stomach cramps and ultimately a miscarriage and the castor oil will help it slip out. I look at the glass; my mother sits back down at the kitchen table. Disconnected from us, she begins to pray. I drink and gulp down the pills. My lips are oily and the mixture is the most volatile, disgusting concoction I've ever swallowed in my life. My sister made the juice with warm water. I have an oil slick around my mouth as I swallow every drop until there are only bits of orange pulp on the bottom of the glass.

The options are minimal; it was this or fly off in a plane with someone who doesn't like me and get married. Just the word marriage makes me think of my mother, always cooking, washing, grocery shopping. She also mops and irons. I don't know how to cook and clean; my mom does it all for us. My father's plan is not about an actual marriage. I would have Tom's last name and be a respectable pregnant girl, our family name saved.

After swallowing the tablets and gagging, I wipe my mouth with a tea towel my mother has embroidered with little blue birds. I follow my sister into the back yard. We play tetherball, and think about our next plan. Bobbie says the rest of it is about Mother Nature. She tells me to trust her, and next comes the easy part. Easy for her to say, and Mother Nature has not been a good friend so far. Bobbie forgets to mention the diarrhea lurking around the next corner.

We find our hula hoops against the house, put them around our waists and begin to move our hips. Round and round and round we go, to get things stirred up. She wants to get my situation resolved and I'm her puppet. I am energized with the thought in my head that my dad will be surprised when I tell them that we took care of the pregnancy. She stops and lets her hula hoop fall to her ankles while cheering me to move it. Coach Bobbie yells for me to move it faster, faster. I am a whiz at this hula hoop game and have great rhythm. I can move my hips like nobody's business. Dancing is one of my best talents. I continue to move my body to music in my head. I used to have contests with friends and I always won. I could keep that hoop up and going around my hips for hours. Round and round and round I go until I start to get diarrhea. I dart into the house just in time, but only have cramps and a bit of back seat rumble.

I return to hear her next plan. We abandon the hula hoop idea and go to Plan B. With my problem still intact, I realize I have cramps in my lower abdomen. We are getting closer to our goal. We decide to run around the block, twice. Off we go past the snotty girls' house two doors down, around the corner next to the fence and the Edison trucks, around the next corner and down one more block past the house of Ann B. Davis, an actress. We sisters run like the wind until we are back home. Panting, red faced, we drink water and then off we go again. We jump up and down, play tether-ball again. Both competitive, this is no longer about aborting. It is about getting the rope from my sister, hitting the ball with all my force to get the rope around the pole and win.

It's one drastic idea after another. Plan C: Bobbie tells me to climb up the trellis and jump off the roof. I carefully climb up the rickety trellis until I get my footing on our roof. I have always been afraid of heights; this is definitely the final hour. My sister stands on the grass in the side yard and yells up to me. "Now jump and get this over with–jump!"

I yell back to her, "Are you crazy? No dice. I'll still be pregnant with two broken legs."

She yells back, "Oh, just jump!"

She is actually getting irritated with me for not jumping off a roof. I can't believe it. I inch my way closer to the edge, look down as I move all the way to the edge with my legs bent for balance. I inch as close as I dare, with my toes peeking over.

I peer down at my sister, notice her long, thick brown hair in a pony tail. I always wanted hair like that...geeze Judi, concentrate, snap out of it! I look at her again. Staring up, she returns my gaze with that look she gets. Her forehead wrinkles and her nose crinkles, and we both start to laugh. She tries to look concerned but it is so funny and we are laughing like big nuts. Neither of us has any sense; me on the roof, her on the ground laughing like the fools we are—two dumb sisters. Our faces are distorted from laughing. I lean back and wail with laughter. We try to regain control of ourselves. Finally with a few deep breaths, we recover from our laughing fit. We continue with my plight.

I stand, take deep breaths and look at her, but this time I really see her, maybe for the first time. She stands on the grass with the hula hoops on the ground next to her feet. She is young, she is not a doctor, she's not even a nurse. She has no idea what she's doing. This is the moment I have my first epiphany. I feel calm. It's crystal clear. I'm going to have a baby and nothing will change this, nothing.

As I turn around to climb off the roof, I hear her yell, "Come back! Where are you going? Just jump, come back!"

I decide at that moment to test her level of devotion and concern, so I yell back down at her, "I'm too scared to do it. Come up here with me and let's hold hands and jump together."

She looks up and yells, "NO! I don't want to hurt myself. I have to work tomorrow."

I carefully walk back across the roof and climb down, slow and with purpose. I'm pregnant. And then it hits me. Not the reality of my pregnancy but the diarrhea, stomach cramps. The insanity of our backyard adventure has finally mixed up the oil concoction. I have to climb down fast. With my butt cheeks held tight I run as fast as I can to the bathroom. I run to the back door, fling it open and tear down the hall, past my mother as she steps out of her bedroom to see what all the yelling is about. I land in the bathroom and slam the door. Just in the nick of time. I have the most horrible diarrhea which lasts forever. I sit here and rock back and forth and moan and hold my stomach in a protective way. I'm sorry for my baby and for me.

Mom brings me a glass of cold water which makes it worse. She places a cold washcloth on my forehead. After an hour or so, I have painful cramps thrown in for good measure. This is out of my hands. Someone else is calling the shots and that someone is a baby. I assume it is happy, content, and loving the yummy mystery drink. I guess I'd better go to the Vogue store and pick out my wedding dress.

Bobbie doesn't want to be around when I'm finished. Her abortion clinic is closed, and I want to strangle her. I always hold her responsible for everything bad in my life. It's our sibling rivalry. I hear a soft knock on the bathroom door. She quietly says bye-bye, and I rock back and forth for the rest of the night.

My mother phones her mother and I hear her praying on the phone with Grandma. Mother walks into my bedroom with a message from Grandma. It's God's will. God works in mysterious ways. This is a lesson. Man can cure disease, but not fate; and let's not forget *Romans 8:28*—"all things that happen are for the good, if you love God and are fitting into His plans."

In my room, I can smell dinner but I'm not interested. Finally my mother brings me a plate of food, pot roast and some of her fresh-cut tomatoes. I try to eat some, but know too well if anything hits my stomach it will shoot out my bottom with a force all its own. I better curl up in a ball and call it a night. For some reason this has happened to me, and no one else. I have no idea why. I am set on a path not of my own choosing and I've lost control of the situation. I never had control in the first place. I guess there's nothing to do but be healthy and try my best not to upset my parents. I toss and turn and try to sleep. Tomorrow my dad will find a place for me to go.

JOANIE

It is a clear, warm day in June. I can still smell the sweet scent of orange blossoms in the air. Everything surrounding me seems unusually still and normal, but it's not. I am spending my last day with a girlfriend. Tomorrow will be my departure into the abyss.

School is out and I need to leave town as soon as possible. I try to hold in my stomach, but it won't retreat back into its proper place. The truth is beginning to expose me. Joanie and I planned to do something spectacular this day. She drives us out of town, east into the foothills to spend the day and enjoy our proud community's new man-made lake, oddly enough named Lake Success.

She drives my car since I'm not old enough to get my license. Cruising along in my well-known blue Opel with our hair blowing wild and free, we each have an arm dangling out the window. We take a few chugs of soda with peanuts dropped in the bottle as always. She cranks up the radio to hear the Four Seasons sing *Sherry Baby* as we zip along past some old people. We sing as loud as we can. Life can't get any better than today. It's a sizzling hot one. Lake Success is situated eight miles east of our hometown of Porterville, with California's Sierra Nevada range as a backdrop.

We drive along and see rolling yellow hills; no shrubs, no trees, just dry scrub brush. We'd heard gossip about a few drowned rattlesnakes, which is unnerving. Okay, actually there was only one dead snake floating in the water. Someone saw it last weekend. But, see one, see twenty.

Joanie turns onto a dirt road and we continue on toward the blue sparkling water in the distance. We park in an open dirt area and with each step we take care as we watch our surroundings, keeping a keen eye out for displaced rattlers. There isn't a snake in sight, and oddly no people, no boats, no umbrellas. No sign of life in any direction.

We make our way down the dirt path to the water's edge and the refreshing sounds of water slapping the muddy shore. We toss the inner tubes into the murky water, walking out deeper with mud squishing between our toes. We flop down and begin to float. The sun beats down on our hot rubber inner tubes. We splash our tubes to cool them down and paddle in circles as we try to maneuver the tubes and stay close together. We talk about life, not the life growing inside of me, but of shared stories as we know them. Our conversations have the same depth as if we were looking at the sky through a reed. Our range of experience is limited and our stories repeated many times.

Joanie likes me to sing to her and I happily comply. We float and bounce in the water and I sing my heart out. She listens, and as usual she tells me she likes my voice. I know she loves me because I actually sound like a cat with its tail caught in the door. Thank God we haven't seen any rattlesnakes, alive or dead.

A light breeze brushes across our bodies just enough to keep us cool. The sun beats down on our backs and legs. What a wonderful feeling. Contentment fills this moment; finally I have peace of mind. I'm still an innocent and carefree teenager. No looks, no whispers, only me and my friend. Joanie mentions she can see a little pouch starting to show, and she musters up the courage to ask me how I feel about being pregnant. I am honest and tell her I'm worried, embarrassed, and scared of the unknown. Neither of us knows how a baby comes out, or the process. We've both heard about labor, but we have no idea what it means. We decide it's cramps, really bad cramps. I tell her I can handle that and we agree I am in good shape from being on the swim team and have no worries. The final assessment is bad stomach cramps, then a baby.

The biggest problem for us is the story line. Joanie is my front man. She has to tell lie after lie in response to questions and concerns pertaining to my whereabouts. Joanie is not a liar and I know she'll mess up, so we rehearse this question and answer skit over and over. Once again: "Judi is in Seattle at the World's Fair." I remind her not to look anyone in the eye, turn and leave. Once again, say it and leave.

I have no idea what I think about my situation or what I'm going to do. I take great pride in being tall and skinny, and although a few weeks ago I was told I'm pregnant, deep down in my soul I'm pleased because I've finally begun to fill out and have a good figure like my mom. In my head I'm confused. The thought of giving birth is so far beyond my comprehension I can't grasp the concept. I only found out where babies come from a few years ago.

We trudge out of the lake. In an instant our bodies are dry and hot. I reach in and grab my camera off the dashboard. At the same time we both notice dust flying in the distance, coming in our direction. We're isolated as we stand there in our bathing suits and wait. Up and over the hills we see a truck, surrounded by brown dirt clouds. Closer and closer it moves and bounces over rocks, sometimes visible, sometimes not. Closer it comes, and then up again as the cloud flies over rolling hills, then it's upon us.

Relieved to see a familiar face and not a murderer, it's Maurice, a senior from our high school. He sees us and stops. We ask him if he would mind taking a picture of us in the water while we float on our inner tubes. No problem. We jump back into the murky water, run farther out and pose. We yell for him to wait a second because we decide to drop down to our necks in the water for privacy. Maurice waits patiently and then he snaps us, puts my camera down on the hood of my car, and off he goes. His long arm waves goodbye as dust engulfs him.

The cold, dark water is refreshing as small waves hit our backs. This gives us delusional thoughts; we are at a swank resort with no worries. We float for hours without much conversation. We paddle and our arms aid us to control our position. Close to the shore is soft silt from the freshness of the dam construction. This water is brown like chocolate milk. It feels soothing on my throbbing big toe. I've been so nervous, I clipped my toe nail back too far; now I think it is infected. We get adventurous and go farther out, bouncing and frying our youthful bodies as we float along like fat ducks with no particular place to go.

Joanie is almost as tall as me, with black wavy hair and green eyes and a dimple in her chin. She is precious and sweet. I, on the other hand, have brownish-red hair, light blue eyes, and a big nose. I am skinny despite my advancing condition. She is soft-spoken, shy and private, yet manages to be in all the class plays and is the editor of our year-book. My only accomplishment is being a fast swimmer and funny.

This is the perfect day before I leave. Neither of us has any idea that today, this day, June 18, 1962, floating in water, chatting and laughing, confessing our secrets and our dreams, will be our last day as young, carefree, boy-crazy girlfriends—friends who practice make-up tech-niques, learn how to go from young girls to grown-up girls. Joanie and I experience this transition hand in hand. But, Judi-girl decides to whiz ahead into adulthood. Everything will change for us, no matter how we fantasize about our future. She wants us to be neighbors someday. I'll be lucky if I can find my way back home.

I close my eyes and feel warm and comfortable as my inner tube bounces up and down in rhythmic motion. Oh yes, I could sleep here all day and then some. I will be tan with a fresh set of freckles when I arrive in my new home away from home. I love Joanie and her support and her unconditional love. This feeling of being safe and happy today is truly necessary for my peace of mind. I have been in denial, and what a wonderful state that has been. Tomorrow will surely bring me out of this utopia and a new world will unfold. This summer will be a chance for me to show my inner strength.

Six months into my pregnancy.

OAKLAND

It's time. Today is the day I leave town like a thief in the night. It's early; we get into the Opel without making a sound. I climb into the back seat, cleverly place myself behind my mother. My father can't see me in the rear-view mirror. Our big brown family suitcase is in the trunk full of maternity clothes my sister Bobbie has sewn for me.

Off we go, the tainted family, the family with the little wench of a girl in the back seat. I lean forward and whisper to my mother. She listens, drops her hand to her side and I hold on. My father's only purpose in life is to get his youngest daughter out of town and out of sight. He veers onto Highway 99 North. Away we zoom toward Fresno. The farther away we drive, the more anxious I feel. The closer we are to Oakland, the smaller I become.

My mother is sad but helpless; my father is quiet and tense. This will be a long ride. He is mad at me for disrupting his life. He's not only hurt, he's betrayed. I glance down at my right hand and touch my ring. Bobbie loaned me her gold ring to wear for the summer.

He stops at one of my favorite places. Now we can rest and have refreshments. I spot this place way down the highway; it looks like a big, round orange ball on the side of the road. This orange round thing has an orange awning with an orange stick to hold it up. Everything is orange. We politely wait our turn, watch the girl squeeze and scoop out the ice. We take our fresh-squeezed orange juice with chipped ice and a straw and get back in the car.

Off he goes like a mad man on a mission. I try not to slurp or crunch ice. The best thing I can do is be quiet and invisible. My father seems to be happier the farther away we get from our hometown. He points out landscapes to my mother. He's always nice to me, but lately he doesn't look me in the eye or smile. I am a huge disappointment to him, but not as much as I am to myself.

We exit off 99 North and head toward San Francisco. We drive across the northern tip of the massive San Joaquin Valley and the rolling hills are greener than our valley hills. The sky is full of fluffy white clouds and I see towns sprouting up.

The traffic is getting heavier. I observe large buildings, rusty industrial roofs and old structures. I see a stream of smoke coming out of huge concrete stacks. There are large parking lots full of old cars and trucks. I see many apartments scattered across the hills. The backdrop of Oakland in the far distance is rolling green hills spotted with beautiful homes. We've been on the road for four hours. I see an exit sign that reads Fruitvale Avenue; he takes it. I click into my memory bank and remember this name, in case I need to find my way back home.

My father turns right onto a side street named Garden Street. I'm glad my spot in the car is behind my mom. I have a good view and can see the landscape, a curving uphill driveway with a sign that reads, "One Way Out." I put my face to the window and look up to the tall stone building. It has a million windows and a wrought iron balcony. It's welcoming and reminds me of Tara in *Gone with the Wind.* This can't be so bad. I see wide concrete steps that go on forever with a black wrought iron hand rail going up the middle. The grounds are smothered with lush landscape, beautiful Japanese trees and pines. I sigh with relief; it's better than I imagined.

We park at the curb at the base of the steps. Mother helps me out of the back seat and my dad gets the suitcase. We walk up the endless, steep steps to the wide doors. Once inside we are in the reception area. Father stands at the glass window and waits; Mom and I sit together. She looks down at my hand and in a soft voice tells me that my gold ring goes on my left hand. I switch fingers and we continue to wait and hold hands. Father reads the rules and talks to the lady. I hear him tell her I have an infected big toe. He asks her more questions, signs papers. Then she comes out to the reception area and tells us to say our goodbyes. I hug my mom and kiss her cheek. I hug my dad and he hugs me back. I look back at them as I leave the wide opening into the unknown. My mouth is dry. I follow a stranger.

I'm in a sleep-walking trance as we walk along the hallway. I hold onto our family's suitcase, which brings me comfort and security. She and I move along the wide corridor, me and the woman from behind the glass window. She tells me to address her as Lieutenant. Red flag. Our soft steps take us closer to my summer home. Quietly we walk, me and the Lieutenant. When we reach Room 4, she hands me the rules of the Home and a key for my narrow closet. She introduces me as Judi G. and leaves.

Three girls stare back at me. I look around the room at strangers. These are the girls I will be sharing my life with during the summer of '62. I stand there with my best poker face, knees trembling and unable to swallow. I pretend to be as calm as a scared girl can be. I don't want them to have a clue about my inner feelings.

My eyes take a quick inventory. I see two colored girls and a white girl. A small nightstand and lamp separate my bed from a girl who lies there and stares. She looks like she is ready to have her baby today. She's grumpy. She is large in the middle and has no need to make a new friend. She stares back at me with no expression. Her rejection isn't racial; it's her time and she has no inclination to be on a welcoming committee.

The other girl, Gayle, is kitty-corner from my bed. She is propped up leaning against the wall crocheting with speed I have never witnessed before. She smiles. She seems to be joyful in spite of where she is. Gayle has short, messy, mousey-brown hair. Her eyes are kind. Gayle has a cute turned-up nose and a sweet face. I sense she was plump before she became pregnant. I'm relieved that she exudes comfort.

My visual exam moves on. These girls seem no different from me, except they are nestled in for the summer and seem content. I always rely heavily on first impressions. I smile back at Gayle. She responds with a cheerful hello and sums me up and down. She continues to pull yarn through and wraps it around her crochet hook again. She keeps a keen eye on me and never skips a stitch.

I look toward my third roommate. Her bed is at the end of mine. Only about four feet separate the end of my bed from the end of hers. This is the one I will be staring at all summer. My third roommate is smiling from ear to ear. She has a twinkle in her eye; she has been waiting for a girl like me. I'm toast. She has shiny black hair with a smooth sweeping bang and her hair is pulled slick back. Her long dark legs go on forever. She is sitting with her back against the wall and her feet almost hang off the end. She's stunning with her beautiful bronze skin, small thin nose, high cheekbones. She winks and asks my due date. This bold question throws me off my first impression game. I quietly mutter, "September 22." She introduces herself as Beth. She's bored and she just found a target, me. That wink tells me she is trouble; the kind of trouble I like.

I begin to sort my clothes and they watch. I put my stationery on the side table with some pens. They watch me like two hawks on a road kill. I look at the girl next to me; she couldn't care less if I danced on the bed or set the room on fire. I carefully put my pink floral mumu on a hanger and Beth giggles and says, "Nice outfit."

Now the game begins. I pull out more and hold them up to me. I show her the pants my sister fixed by cutting out the stomach and tying the sides with shoe laces. This outfit is called, "room to grow." The faded pink floral smock with bouquets of roses is a great hit. She laughs and I continue. Gayle smiles and twirls the baby yarn around her fingers and pulls the hook, watches and waits for the next outfit. I have them with my wit and they need to be entertained, a match made in heaven. I finish with my comedy routine and sit down to look over the rules. Beth says I have plenty of time to read that junk. She suggests we go for a walk and she'll show me around the place.

Beth makes fun of my freckles and my red hair. My hometown in the heart of California is her main target. She considers me a country girl, asks if our roads are paved and do we have a crank phone. We share lots of laughs and tease each other back and forth. But I didn't say a word the first time I saw her hair after she washed it. I stared in disbelief and watched as, holy cow, her hair went from nine inches long to one inch. It was curly and looked like a black ball of yarn. I watched her as she carefully combed out her tight curls, interlacing with gel to help with the tangles. She combed and separated her locks with patience and expert hands. Beth rolled her hair around pink sponge rollers all over her head, popped on a night cap and we chatted like it was any other day. I got to see something new and I sucked up the visual and the process she went through.

My first day here, though, all I saw was her beauty and her dark skin. As time progressed a friendship blossomed. I begin to see her inner beauty. I love the sound of her low sultry voice and sexy giggle. She is my companion and trusted friend. I begin to cling to her for friendship and strength. I like that I can be contrary and openly complain about the food and daily life. It makes her laugh. I am play-acting as if this is a summer fort, like the one my dad built in our chinaberry tree, but this is no fort. All fifty girls living here are living a lie just like me. We try to be happy as we count down the days, each with dread in a corner of our hearts.

This summer is life's journey, from a gawky teenager to a woman. True in theory, but when summer's over, I'll still be a gawky teenager with issues. I'm learning lessons of life, work ethics, and life in confinement. I'm exposed to many disturbing graphic scenes, not for young girls' eyes. I prepare for the unknown without any guidance from anyone. I'm not referring just to the fifty girls housed here with me; I'm talking about the fifty thousand that were here before me and the ones to follow. The same number multiplied over and again across the States, girls who have no choice but to enter through the front door and leave out the back. Girls leave without their babies, to re-enter a world of innocence. We girls stand together, and one by one we take our turn.

The Home is here to house us, hide us, and feed us. This statement is printed on the brochure. The adoption agencies are here to find families for our babies. The medical staff keeps a watchful eye on our health and the babies' health on a rotating basis. There is no one in the middle, dead space as they say on the airways. There's no one to guide us, protect us, console us or prepare us.

Reflecting, I lie on my bed in a home for unwed mothers and dissect my past. I am too young to think about the future; it's too far off. I think about Christmas after Thanksgiving. I think about summer after Easter. My biggest worries consist of my thin eyebrows, my translucent white skin, freckles, my complexion, and the coming weekend. I know what I think of myself—I am not pretty; I'm the tallest girl in school. I have a prominent nose and my eyebrows are a blondish red, just like my hair, and I have my dad's blue eyes. I'm a tall faded girl. But I'm funny, oh heck yes. I can make you laugh.

My sister by comparison has nice dark eyebrows, a nicer nose than me and brownish-green eyes. She has long, thick sable brown hair, a fuller face. I think she looks like Audrey Hepburn. Then there's me, long dangly arms and legs too long and too skinny and I'm too silly and ask too many questions. Most things strike me funny and I seem to be able to make friends easily. But one thing I don't have is a boyfriend or a date. Attending dances is torture; I'm never asked to dance. I've only been to one prom, and I had just seven days notice because my date had been dumped for someone better.

Naturally I want to be loved, noticed, and I want to have someone care about me. I know I have good rhythm and can dance better than most of the short girls on the dance floor. Knowing this is crucial in understanding what it's like to stand on the sidelines and watch. It's like watching a high school marching band with each one out of step. No one wants to dance with a tall girl. A quick mind and wit are no ticket to boogie.

My girlfriends are all experiencing growing pains. We watch each other develop curves and we begin to feel different. We have slumber parties and talk about boys and kissing. Naturally, no one admits to French kissing, except Joyce who wants to practice with us. We wear cinch belts that give us a waist and set off our hips: more curves, more dates. I boss most of my friends around because I'm tall. I realize some of my friends are smarter in class, but I have ideas.

When I began to party and drink liquor, my life began to change. We band of girls weren't content at slumber parties; we wanted to be noticed by the boys. We looked for boys and parties, and the hunt was on for boy-girl interaction. Every weekend I was out with friends and got more creative. A social monster opened its mouth and I happily jumped in. Drinking, honking, waving, yelling, and being in a group at the local Snow White fast food drive-in, being inebriated and getting sick; what fun memories. The social weekend lasted until Sunday when we girls related stories of the night. Dragging Main Street gave me an edge because I'm sitting down and we're all the same size. We cruise to Visalia for new guys and more cars full of kids. The movie *American Graffiti* was filmed not far from my home town, and our town was exactly like the movie.

Now, sitting with my swollen, rolling, live stomach, I have hours each day to think about my situation and my path and where I am today. I can't remember my New Year's resolution.

I'm horrified my friends will find out where I am and why. Being in trouble doesn't mean the simple words, she's pregnant. It means I had sex, and that is the worst part of the truth, the dirty truth. I feel dirty; I am dirty. I have shamed my family and hidden my wanton ways from my friends. I wish I could take back that night. It was dangerously irresponsible of me. I never considered the consequences. I had never known a woman who had a baby and not been married. I thought it took a lot of time and experience. I have learned a huge lesson—it does take time. Less than a minute .

Who would ever have dreamed I would birth a child before I could drive a car?

The rules of the Home are not to be broken. There are strict guidelines to follow and chores to do and the impending birth to worry about. Here I sit in this confining, suffocating, rigid atmosphere, housed with strangers. Indeed, this building is a hiding place. This impressive three-story building is a great place to vanish from sight. The building conveniently has a medical facility on the third floor. In this building there is also a school, a church and a full kitchen and dining area. It's completely self-contained for covering shame. We girls and our social mistakes should be happy to have a place to disappear and have our babies. A young unmarried girl cannot stay at home and have her baby, that's out of the question. Abortions are illegal. You cannot be in public, pregnant and unmarried. Unacceptable. Life is as simple as that.

This entire summer is more like a dream, a bad dream. I thought this Home would be full of bad girls, naughty girls, girls who sleep around, but it's just the opposite. The Home houses girls from all walks of life and all moral behaviors. Cheerleaders, song leaders, quiet girls, Christian girls and girls who don't wear make-up, hair pulled back, soft and natural. Naive girls and scared ones live here. There are girls from staunch families and girls from families with money and status. This is not a home; it's a hiding place. Without these girls and their mistakes, this place would go out of business. You cannot be pregnant and unmarried and strut yourself shamelessly around town in a smock. There is nothing a girl can do to be safe from this fate except condoms, and no one in their right mind would go to a store and buy one.

It's the 1960s and dancing is becoming more expressive. Jerry Lee Lewis is pounding on his piano hitting the keys with his feet. My parents don't allow me to play his music on my record player. I might get ideas, but I already have ideas from watching *Rawhide* with Rowdy Yates (Clint Eastwood). Couples are dancing closer and more suggestive, and most music reeks of love and sex, from Ike and Tina Turner to the Shirells and Fats Domino, who found his thrill on Blueberry Hill. I'm not a prude, mind you, and not judging; it's just the times, and kids and music are changing. I learned to dance from watching Elvis and American Bandstand. My sister showed me and my girlfriends how to shimmy. I learned quickly, but we only did this at slumber parties. Concentrate, hold out your arms and shake your chest and back real fast.

Blues and rock and roll are taking over. Elvis is grinding his hips with sexy moves I've never seen. Short dresses and miniskirts are becoming the fad. So are open-toed shoes, and going bare-legged without nylons. I still borrow my mother's girdle when I go out because it holds up my nylons and makes me look skinnier, but most girls are going without them. Seems everyone is more aware of their bodies; tight sweaters and matching tight skirts are the rage. In the summer, halter tops, showing off bare backs and shoulder blades, are sold in stores. Knee high boots with short skirts. Everywhere you look it's sex.

There are guys with greasy hair trying to emulate Elvis and girls backcombing their hair to make it bigger and puffy. We wear frosted pink lipstick and lots of black eye make-up and tight copper belts. Girls are aware of their bodies; tight pants and Nehru jackets are the boss thing to wear. But when one of these girls goes too far and misses her period, the music stops.

A Home like the one I am living in this summer is full to capacity. Girls want to get in and hide. There are hundreds of these kinds of homes popping up all over the United States. Most are full and although you have to wait, the wait's not that long. Six months max and you're out. We girls are labeled and it stays with us forever. You will always be the girl who went away.

The Salvation Army that provides these homes stands for truth and charitable deeds, but it seems to me, by housing all of us they must be doing quite well in the financial department.

ANOTHER DAY AT THE HOME

A cool bay breeze moves through the branches of a Chinese elm just outside my bedroom window. The swaying branches lull me into a restful suspension of ease. I am lonely in a building with fifty girls. I watch and remember. I remember my home, my family and my friends. They'll be there when this long summer is over. Beth's low sultry chuckle snaps me out of my time warp. She is amused by an article in a magazine. She continues to read; I wait.

I watch her and surmise the difference between us; she is content because she has a plan. I have always expected someone to bail me out. Now there is no one who can come to my aid. It's too late. My plan was to pack my stuff and head north with my father at the helm. I called Joanie and reminded her to tell everyone I'm at the World's Fair.

Beth's plan is to tell everyone she is away at a secretarial school in northern California. She told her family she will pay the tuition herself. She went on to say she'll live in the dorms and return in late summer. She'll come home with a box of pencils as proof, and me, I'll have to explain why I was at the World's Fair for four months.

The intense gaze I was burning into her magazine must have worked. Beth puts down the magazine, looks across the room and says, "What?"

"Come on Beth, let's do something fun."

With her familiar wide grin she stands, puts on her slippers and says, "Let's go snooping around the place and see what we can stir up."

Off we go, like moths to a flame in search of more adventure. Out of our room with a quick turn to the left past the large roomy bathrooms and a quick right, we are now heading toward the long endless hallway. We walk side by side and always next to the wall. It is a given; no one walks down the center. Perhaps none of us want to appear conspicuous. The floor in the hallway is shiny, wide and intimidating. Most of the other girls gravitate to the wall also; we do it because it makes us feel more secure.

We walk along, not talking, no need. We are the tallest girls living here. Both have long legs and arms and long thin necks. We tend to be proud of what we have and that might have been our downfall. We walk together and resemble bookends, one light and one dark, holding our heads high, shoulders back with a mystique of confidence, but it's all an act. We are young and we are frightened. We follow the rules, like all the others, but we're not sure why. This Home has strict rules; at 6:30 A.M. the Major comes by and knocks on each door to wake us up.

Breakfast is served at 7:30, lunch at 12:00, dinner at 5:00, lights out at 10:00. Sometimes we wait, count to ten, and meet in Room 2 and dance. Man, those colored girls sure can dance.

Beth and I turn down the wide concrete steps and into the basement. There we find other girls searching for something to do. Some girls walk out of the laundry room, others mill about with no purpose in life except to kill time. We pretend to have a reason to be here. Ducking into the laundry room, we're surrounded with the unmistakable smells of hot ironed cotton, bleach and suds. It is noisy with the washers and dryers going full throttle. We separate and talk to girls folding clothes or ironing. Both of us gravitate to the other side of the room where racks of free clothing wait, left behind by girls who have returned to their lives.

Beth puts her fingers on top of the clothing. With great care her fingers begin to judge the material, her long dark fingers perform a high step, and one by one they march along the tops of each item. The analysis complete, her fingers have reached the end of the clothing inspection. I reach for an orange paisley top with tucking at the bra line. It is so cute, and I've had my eye on this one for three weeks. As the girl grew larger so did my desire to wear her smock. Beth makes sure all the smocks are in order, all facing the same direction. Any other time in her life she wouldn't waste time scrutinizing used clothing. With my new top folded in hand, we leave the basement with its dull eerie lighting, giving off the illusion of a secret underground tunnel.

We walk straight down to the other end toward the dining room. Through the door we see the same five girls performing the same chores: preparing the same foods, setting up the same tables, carrying the same chairs, placing the same silverware in the same spot. Today is no different from any day; you can put your money on monotony. We sit and wait, resembling birds in a nest waiting for a worm. Our staples consist of loads of butter, piles of white bread, gallons of juice, glasses of milk and mounds of salt and pepper, all for our babies. Time to eat. All fifty girls are accounted for and the Lieutenant stands. We follow her lead, stand behind our chairs, and recite a prayer in unison—the same prayer we have said every day, three times a day since our arrival.

Back upstairs in our room we sit and decide the best and most logical thing to do is rest. No hopscotch today; the weather is overcast and cooler than usual. I first hang my slightly used orange top in the closet, lie down and take a deep breath. Beth mentions how thin I am. This is a caring observation; no one else would have noticed. The food is not what I am accustomed to. Beth tells me how much she likes the food and reinforces the fact that they are good to us and we have a nice place to live.

I have my own thoughts on this subject. The fattening food they shove down our throats three times a day is not what I am used to. I keep this to myself. After a few minutes I tell her I have lost seven pounds since I arrived and I am supposed to be gaining, not losing. She looks concerned, but says nothing.

My thoughts about the food and my lack of appetite lead me to daydream of my mother. I admit that my mother spoiled me. My mother's perfection in the kitchen consumes my thoughts. My mouth waters at the thought of her crispy, golden fried chicken, each part cut perfectly into the same size and always with the breast of the chicken and wishbone set aside for me. I could use a wishbone right now, that's for sure. Beside her chicken, she always serves a side of mashed potatoes, no lumps, with a dent from a large spoon in the center where a tab of butter starts to melt. On the edge of the plate are tomatoes, with their unmistakable vine-ripened flavor, the pattern of red alternating with green avocados. I didn't appreciate her cooking until now.

Beth wants to know what I'm thinking; I have a slight smile on my face. I tell her it's all about my mother's Southern-style cooking and I continue to smile. She seems to think I'm funny and laughs like a mad woman. I am sure I'm the one who will push her over the edge and drive her crazy. For some reason I make her laugh every day, even when I am attempting to be serious.

Beth is beautiful; she has no idea. She has this perfect face, a wide grin with perfect white teeth, a sexy low voice that crackles when she talks, and her hair, that hair of hers is never out of place, perfect every day. She is my first colored friend. Not many colored people live in the valley where I live, and we tend to stay with our own anyway. I don't understand this, but this is how it's always been. White girls don't want to hang out with colored girls and I'm sure the feeling is mutual. I am in awe of her strong self worth and her discipline. Beth never seems to flinch at life's curve balls. She takes it in stride while I, on the other hand, feel I am being punished and a prisoner of my own mistakes.

Beth is the only person who makes me feel safe here. She doesn't judge me and she is easy to be with. Her mischievous chuckle has a calming effect on my high-strung nature. She sees the good in every situation, and I only see the shadows. I am suspicious and cautious. I suspect they are fattening us up to get our babies.

After our rest and digest segment, we tire of lying around and try to rustle up something to do. From our room we hear noise down the short distance to the parlor where many of the girls have congregated. A small television with a black and white screen blares out the sounds of a *Jetsons* cartoon. We missed *I Love Lucy*. No seating left, we move on. Next on our agenda is mandatory chapel in thirty minutes. Beth saunters over and talks to the other colored girls sitting at another table. I walk straight for the French doors at the back of the room. Swinging the doors open, I step out onto the balcony, not to jump, although that would fix the problem. I take in a deep breath and enjoy a few cherished moments of freedom and solitary thoughts. Someone has a transistor radio and I hear the music of *Green Onions* blasting away as a backdrop, a perfect feeling for this balcony and the breeze. The cool night wraps around my swollen body. I grasp the cold rail, stand there and watch the sights and let my mind disappear into the evening. The balcony is my refuge.

Outside these walls is a different feeling. I love the location, with a magical view of the Bay and the quaint homes sprinkled about on the foothills, lights dancing in the distance. This is my new home away from home. After a short time a chill comes over me. I step back into the parlor, tip my head toward Beth and we saunter down the main hallway for our bi-weekly prayer and sermon. Usually during the serious part of the sermon she'll poke me in the ribs with her elbow, or put her fingers together and do a "shame, shame, shame on you." We listen, each verse emphasizing sin. The preacher stares down at us from the pulpit. No one dares smile.

Inside the Home I'm keenly aware of my surroundings. This three story building is beautiful and peaceful on the outside, foreboding on the inside. The entire building gives off a negative charge, one I am acutely aware of. I have never felt this shadow of doom before. This unseen dark cloud keeps me alert. Beth and I stick close together as always, and continue to walk close to the wall. If she is feeling the same doom as me, then she is a great actress. I can only assume she mulls over her situation as she waits for sleep to weigh down her eyes. We each have our own cross to bear.

DARK DAY

Days pass and I begin to come alive. Beth gives me space until I'm able to work through my feelings. It is a slow transition back to my playful spirit, but I soon begin to enjoy each day. During my dark time the parlor had seemed like a glass tomb, but with needed rest and self-reflection, the parlor begins to appear in a different light. It is an inviting area to read, watch television, dance, exercise. The balcony, my safe place, still beckons me. We wait for the birth of our babies and renew our nightly chats and dances. Nothing changes. Chapel twice on Sunday and once on Wednesday evening, all with the same sermon: sins of the flesh, honor thy father and mother, and tend to your daily chores.

At night, the Major comes around and knocks on each bedroom door to let us know we have lights out in ten minutes. Exactly ten minutes later, lights flicker, and darkness takes over. There are many nights I wish I could stay up late, listen to my transistor radio or talk to the girls. I know with fifty girls living under one roof, rules are necessary. There are a couple of girls on the second floor I would not want to meet up with while roaming around in the wee hours.

Girls living under the same roof in close quarters is a disaster waiting to happen. In a less emotional setting, this type of confinement would lead to mood swings and bickering, but when all of the girls are pregnant and in deep trouble, temperaments stay mellow. Everyone wants to do their time and return home. This environment also colors the days in shades of gray. We are boring girls hiding our true selves with our personalities on hold.

In the beginning, showering was a sea of bellies and quiet girls going about mundane personal grooming routines. In slow motion, and as the weeks crawl along, new arrivals find their groove and slip into a slot for personal attention. We take turns, mornings or evenings in the shower station. I am depressed for months and manage to take a shower three times a day. I stand in the stall and let warm water run over my distended body, my sore back and head. I close my eyes and let the water run all over me, engulfing my face and chest. Eyes closed, I pretend I'm home. No one notices or orders me to get out; no one calls me a water hog. If anyone is looking for me, they look in the showers.

What a sight to behold in the showers after breakfast and in the evenings. Our floor houses twelve girls, four to a room. At any time you will find three to ten girls in the restrooms, primping, looking at their profiles, trying to bend over and shave their legs, but not me. Being tall has its advantages. I haul one leg over the sink and stand like a flamingo and shave. Most girls are modest; they step into a shower stall, then take off their robes and hang them on a hook outside the curtain. Many times I saw pregnant bellies, a girl with a towel around her hair trying to put on a robe.

It's our grooming time that brings us closer together. In silence we secretly check each other's stretch marks. This is the only way we can witness our own bodily changes and assess what is normal. This is our only gauge. In the beginning when I first arrived, I used to watch Beth undress, mostly out of curiosity. I had never seen a colored girl naked, but after a couple of days, I decide her body is no different than mine. We groom ourselves with the others as one big family.

Evenings can be fun, and also depressing. We dance or gather in one of the rooms and sit on beds to chat, but this can only last for so long. There are times I desperately need alone time, time to think and time to comprehend my situation. If I need to withdraw I am either in the shower or curled up in bed or standing on the balcony.

I wonder about my friends I left behind. I wonder about my future and how the friends back home will treat me. I never told Rita; I couldn't bear it if she dumped me. The fear of the delivery is pushed to the back of my mind, but always there. When this is over, the most important thing for me is acceptance.

I lie on my twin bed and listen to the music that stirs me into thinking there is still true love out there. My baby turns and moves until it is comfortable. I worry about the baby and how it will grow up with or without me. The song *Stagger Lee* comes on the radio, my sister taught me how to jitterbug to this song. With my eyes closed I can see us dancing; one foot to the left, then put that foot back to the other foot, step back and repeat. Listen to the beat she would to say. Go *Stagger Lee*. I am in heaven and so delighted to hear this song. One day I will be back home and I can jitterbug with my sister and girlfriends on our hardwood floor. Sleep is coming; I turn off the radio just as the Major sticks her head in and says, "lights out." Goodnight sister.

Days seem to last forever, chores never end and this will be the longest summer of my life. It's amazing, the irony of it all. The boy who did this to me is guiltless, and on to the next chapter in his life. He's moved out of town, is dating another girl and has no worries, except the wrath of my father. Boys don't seem to have an attachment to a baby like we do, and they won't have the pain of delivery. This is so unfair. I am trying not to hate boys as I lie here and wait. I wonder if I will ever in my life have a normal relationship and if I will ever have real sex, the type of sex people have when they are in love and it's okay. I doubt if I will ever do that again. I think I might be without a boyfriend until I'm thirty.

I know one thing for sure. I'll be a scared little rabbit if I go out at night. Joanie has Bill, and when I return I have decided to stick close to Rita and Murray. They don't care about boys and they are fun. They don't go to parties either; we make our own fun when we are together. Rita is like a sister to me, and we have great times together. I remember lying in her bathtub encased in bubbles with my head back on the tub while she played classical songs on her grandmother's baby grand piano. I'd yell for her to play like the giant in *Jack and the Beanstalk* to antagonize her. Then she would hit all of the keys at once and yell for me to get out of the tub. Oh, how I wish I had her claw-foot tub and piano music today. Rita likes to act angry, but she never is. The three of us are into athletics and driving fast with the wind in our hair. When I return home it will be no hassles and no boys. With memories of Rita's music and bubbles, I feel sleep taking over my thoughts.

Next day I am rested and ready to do my chores and continue on, and not lose my sanity like yesterday. I saw a girl today in the hallway, walking from the mothers' ward down toward the opposite end of the hall. She looked like a monster, a dead stare and her hair was a mess. She walked real slow with her legs apart. Her hand was on her stomach, like she was holding it up. This monster girl scared me more than the smell of disinfectant. I wanted to speak to her, but as she walked, her eyes looked straight ahead. I wonder what happened to her.

Beth is my only refuge. She gets depressed and bored too, but she hides it better than me. Beth keeps her cool and has her spunk, and she stays focused. She prepares her body and keeps her hair looking good, and she keeps her cards close to her chest.

I learned this card trick when I played poker with old men at a park who lived in the cabins supplied by my grandfather. I sat under a trellis and we'd play slap jack or poker. I was five years old when this started. My mother was the cleaning lady for the cabins. Mother kept a close eye on me as I slapped the stack of cards, and the old guys always let me win. I know about keeping those cards tight and out of sight. Right now I would rather be sitting with a bunch of grandpas with whiskers than here, in this room the size of a jail cell.

Well, as the old folks say, "You play, you pay." I am here because I am weak and I was bad. I'm a girl in trouble and I need to pay the price and endure the shame and go through great pain and discomfort like the monster girl in the hallway. I know clearly why I am here and it's entirely my fault. I can't get angry at the Home for housing me; I can't get angry at my friends for having fun this summer. I want to scream, I am so mad at myself. I had it made; a nice home, food in front of me, friends, cute car, and look what I did. I pretend it is just one summer out of my life, but this is a huge big deal. When I mess up, I do it big.

The radio is playing Ray Charles again and I am sick to death of this song. Finally, dinner is announced. At least I will have something to do for an hour. The last meal was yucky. There was blubber on my meat and it was so gross I wanted to gag. I picked at it, dug out as much as I could and then pushed it to the side. Who serves blubber and why? I am in a bad mood and need to eat normal healthy food and not slop. I wonder if the cook is a transfer from a state prison. I will shower again and get into bed. Beth stays her distance when I am in a dark place like today.

CHORES AND LETTERS FROM HOME

Another day begins like all the others, but I notice there are more empty beds. I see the new girls arriving, but never see anyone leave. It's a revolving door of youth and lost souls.

The letters arriving weekly from Joanie are a welcome detour in my mind. She tells me all the news about our friends and family. No matter how trivial they seem her news perks me up and puts a smile on my face. Each day when the mail arrives I wait and hope my name is called. My mother writes sad ones, my sister writes encouraging ones with stories of her love life, my dad writes about the facts and never mentions the baby. Dennis writes different things about our other set of friends with the visual scenes he describes so well. His letters make me laugh. I also get letters from Trudy and my cousin Sharon. The words from my family and friends are devoured in minutes. Each one leaves me with a wave of different emotions. The words from home make me connect with who I am, or was. I feel warm inside while I read, but they can't take me home. I read and remember from a distance. I think of my hometown and the deep friendships waiting for my return. I read my letters aloud to the girls I have bonded with. We live in a state of memories and continue to live in hiding.

My bedroom with my three roommates has become my sanctuary. I lie down, put on a pair of my knitted slippers and turn on my transistor radio. I have knitted thirteen pairs of slippers this summer. I close my eyes, put my hands on my stomach and listen to Elvis, then some rock and roll songs. Ray Charles can't stop loving me. I close my eyes and see my friends' faces, laughing and talking, putting on make-up. I remember the last day before I left home, just me and Joanie. I think of the sweet scent of orange blossoms. I am obsessed with letters from home. I write to Joanie and draw pictures of my hair. I draw diagrams of the Home, all three floors, and write in each room number and the location. I beg her not to forget me and to still be my friend. I try and write cheerful letters, but it is all an act, a double-edged sword. I want to go home, but I can't be seen.

This summer has also been difficult for my parents. My mother lives for her children. My father, who loves us, also loves his status. He climbed up the ladder to success while my mother nurtured us girls. I can only suppose what has transpired while I have been here. My mother is depressed and worried about my condition. My father insists I put the baby up for adoption; my mother wants me to keep my baby.

A month after I arrived I received a letter from my mother saying she and my dad have filed for divorce. I hope this is not my fault. I feel guilty for their separation and divorce. My mother is uneducated; she worries about me and she also has some mental issues from a seizure she suffered when I was fourteen. She had a stroke when I was three, so naturally my pregnancy has taken its toll on her mental health. Mother has no idea how to cope with stress. I hope she has a good attorney. My father, on the other hand, wrote me that he rents a room from a man who is also newly divorced. They have a colored woman come in every day to clean and cook dinner. They have a swimming pool and a wonderful social life. I am reading this, such a different story than my mother's version.

Mother, feeling desperate, hired an auctioneer and with an ad in our local paper, auctioned off our maple dining room table and chairs, our brown tweed couch and chair, our end tables, coffee table and our buffet, along with all our chinaware. I hope she still has all of my clothes and my posters of Joanne Woodward, but who knows. They probably went to the highest bidder.

I put my letter aside and sigh. Mother just sold our furniture. I wonder who put her up to this hare-brained idea. My parents are living in two different houses, and I am frozen in time, unable to help. My baby kicks; my stomach rolls around as the baby continues to do somersaults. I put my letter on the table, turn up the radio and listen to the *Duke of Earl* while my baby dances.

Sometimes I read aloud to Beth. She listens and gives me advice. She counsels me in preparation for my return home, like the one-liner I am to say to the guy who did this to me. I tell her about my friends and parties. She thinks we are a bunch of country bumpkins and is shocked by stories that include orange groves, dragging Main Street, and barn dances. Through her laughter I try to explain life in my hometown in the heart of California's agriculture. She has no concept, and the more I tell her about taco feeds, playing ditch in my car, driving and singing in the fog, the more she howls. She is a city slicker. She smiles and comes back with retorts that I can hardly understand through her snorts of laughter. It's a hopeless situation. She wipes the water from her eyes in hysterics and we continue. I mention rodeos and barrel racing to give her more fuel.

Sometimes I tell her personal things and she tells me about her life and family. I look at her and cock my head to one side. We are different, but we like each other and mesh well together. We share our hopes and dreams and the obvious, our regrets. Our friendship has bloomed as much as our bodies. We talk at length about how this is going to end. In plain terms, how does the baby get out? Obviously the same way it got there. A baby is big; this concerns us. No one seems to know. We have heard stories from mothers and aunts, but no one ever told us the real story. There is the allusion to pain, but no one tells us. We all know deep down in our hearts this is going to hurt, but pretending not to know is crucial to our sanity. We hope when summer ends we will return home and regain our self-worth, become the same girls we were before. No one on our floor, or any floor for that matter, seems to know anything about labor. The Home provides assistance from the County for adoption, in addition to food, shelter and medical care. There is no one in the middle who we can talk to and learn from, no one. I wonder how I will get through this summer and come out on the other side as the same girl I was before.

Beth listens and gives me solid advice. Not that she is a scholar; here she sits in a home for unwed mothers and has no plan except to fake secretarial skills when she returns home. Still I listen to her as if she is the messiah. She is older than me by two years; she has graduated from high school and knows the ropes. She counsels me what to say to my friends and how to explain my absence from town this summer. We practice; my comebacks will flow out of my mouth with ease.

Our platoon of twelve girls meets in the corner of the parlor. This is a huge room with the wrought iron balcony and many-paned windows with curtains. Lots of chairs and tables and couches donated from different families fill the space. They must feel pleased to get rid of the ugly things and this cast-off furniture helps us poor souls in trouble. Oddly there is only one small television. Nice linoleum floors with layers of wax buildup and worn patterns and mismatched furniture provide the illusion of security. Girls tend to gather in the parlor to read, write letters, practice dance moves, stare out toward the bay, or interact with others from different floors. There is no emotion here, no arguments, no jokes, no yelling. None of us want a disturbance; we wait for our turn on the third floor.

Marie turns on her radio and Dion sings *The Wanderer*. Perfect. Each girl has a spirit of hope and wants to work her body to get ready for the impending birth and her return home to prove that she is the same girl she always was. We prepare our bodies for the grand finale. Marie shows us how to strengthen our thighs and arms. Barbara shows us what she learned in a modern dance class; I share stretches learned from swim class. We work our bodies until we are exhausted. It feels good to be productive and take an active role in our fate. We each have moments of depression and entrapment, but as we head toward the middle of summer we resign ourselves to the fact that a positive attitude is the correct and only choice. Exercising is a regular event with our group. We meet on Mondays and Thursdays. A schedule of our own making is powerful, and gives us a smidgen of control. Some evenings I do pushups and squats in our bedroom.

The next day we decide to get in better shape. Some of the other girls from our floor join in and we drop to the floor and begin our exercises, each doing a routine learned in P.E. class or a ballet class. We begin doing squats and sit-ups, and I lift weights using books. We huff and let out air, count and give it all our energy. After our makeshift gym class we separate, some of us shower, others go to their rooms to rest. Beth and I come out of the showers about the same time and meet back in our room. I lather my body with cocoa butter and smell of coconut. She lathers herself down with something that has the smell of lavender. We are both content to be taking a higher road and try to stay positive as we forge ahead to our impending curtain call.

Next morning, Wednesday is sheet day; we must awaken by 6:00 A.M., get busy and strip our bedding. Everyone on all three floors is doing the same thing. We put one sheet and pillowcase into the other sheet, tie a knot at the top, throw on a sweater over our night clothes and head down the hallway to the staircase and down into the basement. Each of us moves about more like sleepy monsters from a horror film than teenagers. We all shuffle along, holding on to our bundles. This mandatory bi-weekly rule was a nightmare in the beginning. Now it is a routine. Like leaves going down a drain, off we go to the basement.

Beth and I join the flow. We stand in line next to the wall so others joining the stream can come and go. One by one we hand our dirty sheets to the Lieutenant who writes down our name and room number. We move forward and the Sergeant hands us a stack of crisp, fresh sheets with a bar of soap on top. We are silent.

Off we go, looking like waiters with our piles topped with soap, back up the stairs. We all know what to do; we make our beds with a military fold at the end on each corner. Take the bottom edge, pull the pieces together and pull taut and forward. Take the bottom of that sheet, tuck it under the mattress and with the part you are holding forward, tuck it under the part you just put under the sheet, giving the corners a fitted tailored look. No one talks. We toss our matching blue floral bedspreads over our sheets and off we go. You never know when there will be an inspection.

Like marching penguins we shuffle back downstairs for breakfast. It's another meal of oatmeal with cream, toast with heaps of butter, a bowl of fruit, juice, milk and instant Lipton tea or coffee. After our prayer and meal, fifty girls disperse in many directions. Some go to the smoking room located not far from the laundry room; others go upstairs to the parlor for television or social interaction or tend to their assigned chores. Beth always waits until the smoking room is empty before attending to her chore of wiping down the ash trays, cleaning the tables, adjusting the newspapers and putting the magazines in order. Once I went in the smoking room with her to see what it looked like. I had no idea pregnant girls smoked. I noticed two red leather couches, a couple of overstuffed chairs, a clutter of ash trays and cigarette butts.

The stench of stale smoke, newspapers tossed all over the chairs and floor, made me realize my own chore was not so bad. She has to clean up this room daily.

My chore is to dust mop the hallways on all three floors. Up and down I push, until I have cleaned every speck of dust, then into the elevator to the second floor. I push past bedrooms, examining rooms and offices, then turn around to do the other side and then the middle. Last is the dreaded third floor. I push the wide dust broom past rooms full of girls who are reading or resting. I turn the corner and head down the hallway past the labor and delivery room to the end. This area is called the mothers' quarters. I smell disinfectant and hear babies cry.

One day I am called into the office again and given the chore of a girl who has left. I am to scrape off food from each plate, rinse off the leftover sauces or juices and push the plates along down the counter toward the washer and then the drying girl. I am in the garbage line. No one talks and no one laughs. I am not happy about this change in chores, but I do it three times a day and never complain to anyone except Beth. She has to listen to me day after day as I tell her about the dirty plates and all the food going down the drain. Oddly, she is amused. She laughs and asks me to tell her more and more gross stories about half-eaten chicken or spaghetti mixed with applesauce. I keep this chore for a month. It is a very long time, and I hope I never have to do it again. I have always had issues with food, and this daily chore only magnifies my problem.

NANCY

A breath of fresh air just arrived. Nancy blew in like the north wind. She is tall, blond, has big blue eyes, a beautiful face, nice high cheekbones. She is in the early stages of pregnancy. Her father is a captain of TWA airline and he had her flown in from New York City. She is proud to tell us that she got pregnant on Blueberry Hill. The father of her baby is a friend of her father. She is happy to be in sunny California, no regrets, no worries. We have great times with her. She's in Room 3 across the hall from us. She joins in, dances, plays hopscotch, goes with us to chapel, and then makes faces at us during the sermon. She stands and recites the prayer before meals and winks and blends in like she has been here for months. We dance many nights in her room, and she helps us short-sheet her roommate's bed. Her chore is dusting the parlor.

The mood on our floor has changed for the better. Our small commune of only three rooms on the main floor is alive again. We exchange stories and realize that life is still going on outside these walls. Nancy loves to talk about New York and introduces us to the *New Yorker* magazine.

She listens to my stories about the Central Valley, the Bay Area and life in California compared to New York. I am happy I will have someone who will be with me after Beth has delivered. Our due dates are close together. Nancy is a much needed positive force. She lives with us for only a few weeks, but weeks full of life that whiz by. I love the information I learn from her about the East Coast, things I had not heard before.

Nancy has already had one exam and the attending physician was the handsome Dr. Copeland. She's a very lucky girl. Then, two weeks later her exam doesn't go so well. Things begin to unravel for her. I have my exam the same day, so we stand in line together, shooting the breeze about boys and music. Her name is called and I tell her, "I'll wait for you." I stand there against the wall and she doesn't come out. I ask and no one sees her come out. Finally the door opens and out comes Nancy, red-faced with tears streaming down her cheeks.

We hang onto the mahogony rail and walk down the steps together but she is someplace else. We walk in silence. Once in her room the girls in our section hear that something is going on and we meet in her room. She finally opens up. She tells us the doctor did his routine exam and heard two heartbeats. Nancy is having twins. I am shocked and feeling extra lucky. She cries and says she needs to tell her mom and go home.

This saddens me, but it is the same thing any of us would do. Having your dad as a pilot is a plus; they fly her mom in the next day and she retrieves her daughter. Nancy packs her clothes, gives me a couple of smocks, leaves her magazines, hugs each of us goodbye, which is a nice way to end a friendship, not like a disappearing act like the rest of the girls. Poof, no more Nancy. She is in a panic and leaves swiftly. From the balcony I watch her mother get out of the taxi. She is a tall, beautiful and stylish lady. I watch Nancy give the taxi driver her suitcase and get in. The taxi drives away. The end of her story is a mystery.

A Shopping Trip

Today is the day we usually head down the street to the small corner market. We have five or six girls who go with us. We get on our jackets or a light sweater and wait for Beth who can't go out without a full disguise. She puts on a hat, scarf, sunglasses and a long trench coat, flips her collar up. She does this in case a member of her family happens to stop by or a friend from high school. Beth lives only minutes from the Home.

Off we go with our friends from different floors. This outing fills our need to get away, brings good spirits and chatter, and it's good for our exercise program we devised. The market is about four blocks away, all downhill. When we reach the open doors and welcoming awnings, some of us begin to pick our fruit, squeezing some, smelling others, while the rest of the girls look at nuts and soft drinks. We're careful not to go overboard and spend all of what little money we have from our families.

Beth walks straight over to me, pulls her hat down lower onto her forehead and without looking around says, "That lady over there in the blue coat is my aunt." She asks if she is looking this way. I tell her no, she is over to the side shopping. Beth says she is going to slip out the door and head up the hill. I can come along or stay and shop. She quickly walks out with her head turned to the front of the store. The other girls are notified with whispers, and we all quickly pay and run out the door with our small brown bags in hand.

Beth waits for us around the second corner. We all walk and say little. This is the first and only time I will witness Beth in fear of being seen and her cover blown. The long walk back up the hill takes more energy than we anticipate. Beth is quiet and relieved; she says she won't be going back to the market, ever. This statement reminds me of how little time she has left and how our time together is coming to an end. I look over toward her, walking with her head up with purpose as she does so well. Her trench coat is showing fullness from the inside pushing out. I haven't been paying much attention to her body. She is clearly in full bloom. Dismayed, I'm quiet and walk with the others as I contemplate this loss.

Some of the other girls are quiet also; we are all walking with deep thoughts of our own. Each of us just witnessed the worst-case scenario: being seen and the truth revealed. This is the reason there are no cameras allowed on the premises. I cannot imagine what I would do if I had come that close to being caught. Beth has refused to go there again. She can't take another chance. Our weekly outings and trek to the market will not be as much fun anymore, not without Beth coming along with us. It will never be the same.

The sun is out today, a rare gift. We are teens, full of energy and eager to get outside and find something to do. A handful of girls go into the craft store while others go behind the building sunbathing on the deck. The young gardener snips away at the hedges while he keeps a watchful eye on the sunbathers. He seems to always find weeds to pull next to the deck. We close our eyes and let the warm sun tan our bodies and listen to music, and in the background, clip, clip, clip.

Our group chalks out the patchwork for our daily hopscotch game. We wait for Beth who is the keeper of the chalk. The center of the driveway behind the building is where we play. Beth and I play hopscotch with Marie and Barbara from Room 3. We are all competitive and this simple toss of the rock turns into a full-blown Olympics. We try to out-jump each other's toss, carefully and with skill. It is playful, the jumping is good for our legs, and the winner just prances and announces the champion. We toss, jump, turn around and plant both feet into the squares and continue. One foot, two feet, then up and around we go, too many times to count. Even though we are pregnant, the jumping on pavement doesn't seem to bother any of us. We toss and jump as high as we can and as far as possible. This is great fun and brings back childhood memories.

Two weeks have passed since we last played hopscotch. My competitors are feeling pressure in their groins and between their legs. I don't feel so bad, but I am three weeks behind them in my pregnancy. I continue to disconnect and not relate to their suffering.

Beth walks to the craft store to check on her bunny cookie jar. She has begun to paint his jacket. I smile and ask how she is going to explain coming home from secretarial school with ceramic bunny ears sticking out of her duffel bag. She chuckles with her trademark crackling laugh, but she is too tired to talk about such abstractions.

Marie and Barbara head to the deck; I follow. We find some lounge chairs, lay our heads back, pull up our smocks, expose our bellies and soak in the sun. Marie is Italian and has big round dark eyes and a small turned-up nose. She is feisty and her story of how she got pregnant changes every week. Barbara is low-key. She has no story to share, so after a short time in the sun she goes back upstairs.

Beth's time is growing near. She is pulling away from me and our mundane jaunts around the Home. She is quiet and seems preoccupied. Last week she showed me her stretch marks. I don't have any on my front, just a few minor pink ones on each hip, and a huge wide one at the bottom of my backside. Beth teases me that my butt is going to fall off if I don't stop that big one. No matter how much cocoa butter or lotion we use, we still have stretched and torn skin. My ribs hurt from being stretched. Beth says in a low soft voice that she can feel the pressure in her groin and something round that might be the baby's head. I panic at the thought of her leaving, but dissociate her progress from my own pregnancy. Our days are slow and methodical. We continue to wait, continue to strip our beds, get clean linens, attend chapel, visit girls in the parlor, stand behind our chairs and pray, and we continue to grow.

VISITORS

Today I have a visitor. I am in a panic so I begin to primp and wait. Someone is on their way. In only twenty minutes I hear my name called over the intercom. With a deep breath I get my sweater and look at Beth for reassurance. Marie pops her head out from her room and smiles. Beth gives me a little wink and tells me to have fun. I step into the wide hallway and move with trepidation toward the reception area. Slow steps carry me along the shiny hallway; my legs quiver and my heart races. Quiet as a mouse, I move forward and try not to bring attention to myself.

There is the opening that leads to the reception area. I see the four-foot half wall with its plastic ferns. I enter and quickly step behind the room divider to spy out my guest while hiding my tummy, which well into my seventh month is difficult to conceal. I'm completely shielded from the waiting room, and I have the ferns hiding me up to my neck. I look up and in the middle of the room stands my Uncle Bill. He is my childhood hero. He's handsome, sweet and funny. Bill is married to my mom's sister. He has black wavy hair and blue eyes. His kids are my close cousins. His daughter Sharon is two years older than me. He's my second dad.

He stands. I stand and we exchange small talk over the ferns as I continue to hide. Finally he asks if I plan on standing there all day or do I think I can muster the energy to step away from the planter box and give him a hug. I grow red in the face; my heart pounds. I feel heat coming up to my neck. Boy, is he in for a surprise. My cousin Sharon will be grounded for life when he sees me. I'd rather be struck by lightning than step out from my hiding place. There is no way out of this predicament. I pull my sweater together in front to help conceal my protruding stomach. I drop my head and step away, exposed.

He carefully sets down a big box of candy and puts his arms around me. He says nothing, just a massive, wonderful bear hug and a few pats on my back. He then puts the box in my hands and tells me it's time to jump ship and grab some lunch. I'm relieved with his playfulness. I want to be happy and silly back at him, but I am mortified with embarrassment and shame. I can't get past my obvious state of pregnancy. I am uncomfortable and continue to hide my front, looking straight ahead as we descend the steps to his car.

We stop for deli sandwiches, sit at a small round table by a bay window. He talks about my cousins and the food. He tells me he has packed some stale bread to feed the ducks. His visit is well planned. Back in his car we head to the park and lake, select a bench in the shade, and soon we are surrounded by hungry ducks. We talk about the weather and life, but not the life under my smock. He never mentions the obvious. He doesn't ask about my personal life or my decisions, which is good because I've made none. I just do what I'm told. He tells me that Sharon is going to Kaiser Nursing School not far from here. I think about how I could use a nurse right about now. The sun begins to set and we head back to the Home. He tells me to share my chocolates and to take care of myself, another bear hug. I run up the wide steps to the double doors with the box of chocolates under my arm, careful to conceal my tummy, turn around and wave goodbye and dart inside. Today was bliss, light-hearted and peaceful. I have been seen for what I am. Uncle Bill will report his visit to his wife, she will call my mother, my mother will call her mother, and my ears will burn for a week.

Down the hallway to our room Beth waits. I toss the box of chocolates on her bed and Miss Cool Cucumber flashes a huge grin with a new attitude. She sits up and together we dig through the candy taking a bite off each corner until we find the one we want. Beth and I enter into a full-blown chocolate frenzy. We decide not to share with the others.

So far I have had two visitors. The first was my father. It was in early summer, soon after I arrived when I could still conceal my pregnancy. We went to Lake Merritt and sat on a bench. He talked about his work, the proceedings of the divorce from my mother, his new home with a swimming pool that he shares with a guy from work, and his life as a bachelor. He was very uncomfortable with me, and I was too shy and humiliated to engage in conversation. He never looked at me. We never made eye contact. He talked and tossed skippers across the water. I love my father and he loves me, but my condition is more than either of us can bear. We sat and pretended to be in sync, but it was a painful charade. After an awkward few hours he drove me back to the Home in silence. I had nothing to say as I did not want any attention coming my way, and I didn't want my voice to be heard. I'm sure he has no idea how we are treated, the chores and strict rules. I can imagine he would agree that every girl in here needs this discipline, and I say nothing.

He put his hand under my elbow and walked me up the long concrete steps. He kissed me on the cheek and said, "See ya, doll." I felt like the lowest scum of the earth. His heart was broken. He tried to be there for me, but neither of us was capable of letting go of the obvious. Being pregnant and out of wedlock is the lowest form of life. It is the worst thing you can do to your parents and it puts shame on your family name. I made a mistake and now I have to pay for it.

Many of the girls have visitors. Some have family dropping by on a regular basis, while others meet their boyfriends outside by the curb. They jump in his car and take off for the day. I have to wonder where they go and what they do. Do they actually have sex again, I wonder? If so, he is getting the better half of the deal. I watch these reunions from my perch on the balcony. Cars drive up and the girls are eager to check out at the front desk, jog down the front steps and into their waiting arms. Others hug and cry. Some girls wave until their family or boyfriend is out of view. I stand and watch. I wonder how a girl can be tucked away because of her boyfriend, yet he comes by and sees her and makes her happy. I mull this over with Beth and we ponder the situation. No sooner do we have this chat when her boyfriend calls and asks permission to come by. Beth says no. She tells him to stay away. A girl has her pride.

TOM

There is a handful of us living here with no connection to the charmer we conceived with. The boy I was with decided to leave town. The unfortunate thing for him was that he didn't leave soon enough. He had to face the wrath of my father. A friend wrote me the story after I was safe and out of town. Tom was downtown eating at the crowded local café with friends in the wee hours of the morning when two policemen entered. The story goes like this: the officers went to his table and asked him to state his name. He did. He was asked to stand; then the police turned him around, laid him across the table, handcuffed him and took him away.

The police said, "This is for the statutory rape of ..." then stated my name.

They hauled him off to jail, and I am told that my father met him there the next morning. My father told him he wouldn't press charges, but instead he'd have to pay the tab for my summer stay at the Home.

I had no idea my father would back me like this. I wish he had shown me this fierce love and concern before I went into the arms of an older guy. I was wrong to let Tom coerce me into having sex. I wanted attention, and I wanted to be loved and noticed. Now, noticed I am.

PAPER GIRL

Today I received another note to go to the office. They are going to change my chore again. This is a welcome surprise and relief. Nothing can be as bad as the garbage line. I am not cut out to work with leftovers and dirty plates and half-empty glasses and someone else's discards. Beth still cleans the smoking room.

My new chore is to go to the janitor's closet, get a basket and fill it up with toilet paper and paper towels. I am paper girl. I am to fill the bathrooms on all three floors. First I go to the main office bathroom, then bathrooms on all floors, which includes the labor room. I am fine with going into the labor room as I have matured and I can handle the scene. In the beginning, the third floor frightened me. I have been exercising and I know now to deliver a baby is not a problem. I also have to go into the Mother's Quarters at the end of the hallway. I have swept past the delivery room and also had my toe operated on in there. Scary, but no big deal.

I've never talked to any of the girls who went before me, but I am ready. In fact, this is the strange thing. We eat together, we sleep at the same times, share rooms, live by the same rules. We stand in line together on sheet day, wait in line and stand against a wall for our medical exams, attend chapel three times a week. We learn to dance and we exercise together. We relax in the parlor; we are a family. We're a unit. Then, one day without any suggestion of trouble, a friend is gone, vanished. Usually we realize her absence at mealtime because her chair is empty. Instead of waiting for her, the Lieutenant stands and we begin our prayer. I am sure the Lieutenant knows this particular girl is on the third floor in labor. Our friend is never seen or heard from again. Because we never see her again, we are never able to ask about her labor or her delivery or simply say goodbye. It is very tricky of the staff to keep her away from us. We wait our turn uninformed.

I find this troubling, an empty feeling of consciousness. It is not normal or healthy. Beth and I concoct a plan to say goodbye. I will need to say goodbye and wish her good luck, and she will need me to be there for her. She gives me her senior picture with her address and phone number on the back, and then she tells me her last name. I do the same. Gayle, our other roommate who was the knitter, had given me a picture of herself in a nurse's uniform. She had signed her name on the back also.

The next morning after breakfast and with pleasure we leave the dining room. No more kitchen duty; I am free to go off with the others. Beth smiles as she tells me she is going to be downstairs in the smoking room to clean. Then we can go out back and play around. I go to the janitor's closet, get my basket and fill it to the top. This new daily chore will take longer than expected. I count the bathrooms and look at the small basket; it takes many trips before paper girl gets her act together. Also included in this chore is emptying the trash in all bathrooms on all floors and offices.

The last room to refill is the labor room. I have been in there once before. When I arrived in early June, a young doctor operated on my big toe because of an ingrown toenail. The nurse told me to report to the delivery room. I was apprehensive, but did as I was told. The surroundings were very scary, white tiled floors, tall lamps with wheels and curtains on wheels. The young doctor asked me to sit on the end of the delivery table. He was on a stool and rolled close to my feet that dangled off the end. The nurse pulled over the large lamps and turned them on. The doctor deadened my toe and began to cut. I didn't watch him cutting my toe. I began to look around, taking inventory with my eyes.

I was sitting on the end of the table on a white strip of paper and I saw shiny silver things attached to either side of the end of the table. They resembled stirrups on a saddle. I noted that I was also sitting between brown leather straps attached to each side of the bed in the middle section of the table. Close to the straps on either side are what appear to be silver gearshifts, same as in my car. I wonder why they have straps and a handle. I had to wonder why they would have to strap us down; maybe this was extra restraints for unruly girls. I had been away from home for only one day and now I was here, on the delivery table, on the third floor. My throat was dry, my heart pounding; I was in a nightmare. I don't want to be strapped down.

Recovering from my memory, I push the button and speak into the gold mesh square, "Paper girl." The door unlocks, and the heavy white door opens. The nurse is very busy; she walks in one direction and points in the other. I pretend this room is no different from any other room. It seems like a long time ago when I sat right there on that same table with my big toe mishap. The labor room's bathroom is connected to the delivery room, but on the far side. I am in a position which forces me to walk past the delivery table. I have to slow down and look. This time there is blood splattered on the white tile floor; papers from the table are wadded up and covered with blood. A large pile of blood-soaked towels lies in the corner and some hang out of the hamper. I don't want to see what I am seeing; like you do when there is a fire. A person knows they should keep going, but you stop and look. I quickly load up the bathroom with fresh papers and walk out past the remains of a birth. I can smell the scent of birth, no explanation, no sound; nothing but red splatters on white tile.

The aftermath of the birth makes me dizzy with fear. I am numb, scared, and my eyes tainted for life. I've lived in a world of denial until this scene. I don't want to tell Beth. She is swollen; her ankles are swollen too, and I feel sorry for her at this stage of her pregnancy. The last thing she needs to know is there will be lots of blood. I will keep this horrific scene to myself.

I lie down to think and try to forget. Beth is lying down with her feet perched up on a pillow to help with the swelling. Lost in my bloody thoughts, I say nothing. She asks me if I delivered paper upstairs in the delivery room. I murmur, "Ah-huh." I realize how horribly unprepared we are. We have yet to be counseled. We are walking the plank without a plan.

Finally some excitement comes our way. We lie on our beds writing letters one evening and reading when we hear noises outside our window. Directly outside our window is a platform for the fire escape. All four of us look toward the window and see a bunch of boys looking back at us. We scream, and they laugh and try to scramble back down the fire escape. The Sergeant comes running in and she calls security, which is news to me. We watch as a man we have never seen walks the grounds. Beth gets up and looks out the window toward the boys as they run away. She checks the security of the window and then grabs the curtains and smacks them together like she is angry. Then she turns toward us and belts out a laugh. I go to the window and peek out. I see a man with a flashlight. I guess we have more security than we thought. The girls are excited about the commotion and others are in our room. I sit stone-faced, not amused. We're a freak show.

LEGAL PROOF

All girls are to report to the parlor for a mandatory information meeting. Dinner is over. This must be important; it's our social hour. We have never had a mandatory meeting. Hopefully this meeting will help us with information about our pregnancy, the paperwork and medical knowledge. The room begins to fill with girls. More chairs are brought into the parlor and set up three rows deep in a semicircle. Our speaker arrives late and introduces himself; he begins his well-rehearsed informative speech.

The stranger begins with a discussion about hormones and the discoloration or darkened patches on our faces and necks. He informs us that the patches on our faces are called a pregnancy mask. Beth doesn't have one and neither do I. Many of the girls look as though they have dirt on their necks and faces, or a dark birth mark. He tells us that a pregnancy mask is caused by hormones, but he fails to tell us what the word hormone means. No one seems to know, and he doesn't explain. We are either too shy or afraid to ask.

He continues to tell us about the dark vertical line we are developing on our abdomen. He says each one of us has a dark line located from our belly button straight down to the top of our pubic hair. I glance at Beth and she tries not to burst out laughing at the word "pubic." I have to look away from her and bite my lip. He said the word pubic. Many of the girls snicker or turn pink.

He is undaunted and continues with ease. "This line is most commonly referred to as a Mother Line. It will darken as you get closer to your delivery date."

Without a breath he continues, "This line is legal proof you have had a baby. It will never go away. From this point on you will never be able to wear a two-piece bathing suit. I believe they call it a bikini. If you do expose yourself, everyone will know you have had a baby."

I sit paralyzed. I am fifteen years old and branded for life, and I have a bikini.

He clears his throat and finishes with another tidbit of information, "From this day forward, note. You have been warned. You must prepare a story for your future husband on your wedding night, or he will know. Your P.E. teacher will know, and everyone you swim with will know. Your doctor will know."

This is the entire meeting and it ends with a crushing blow to our futures and our egos; our secret will be revealed.

We don't laugh as we return to our rooms. Beth questions this man and his legal proof. She shrugs her shoulders and blows it off like a piece of lint on her sleeve. I feel like a branded steer. Marie flops on my bed and calls him cuss words. Barbara goes to her room and quietly closes the door. Our beds are crowded with girls, all wanting to talk about this Mother Line. Beth encourages us not to worry; it's not the end of the world.

This nightmare is too much. I have barely had sex, got pregnant, and then was sent away from the safety of my home, family and friends. Now, branded for life. I raise my smock and run my finger down my mother line, stretch my neck out as far as I can and look over my stomach. I see it. There it is, just like he said; there is a brown line. All is quiet in the rooms. The branded girls don't dance tonight.

Coming out of denial, I need time for my emotions to unfold. Beth refers to him as a jerk; she shrugs it off. I am stunned by this medical announcement, thanks to a stranger who dropped the bomb about the dark line. I have it and I am feeling angry for the first time.

Up until now I have kept very quiet and unemotional and nonverbal about my situation. I haven't shown any emotion since the day I was informed I was five months pregnant. Now I go into a kind of trance and become obedient and mute. I want to be left alone; Beth senses my dismay and stays quiet. I crawl under the covers and curl up with the little person inside me. I can feel its tiny elbows cruising my side. I put my hands on my baby and we fall asleep.

Days pass and we begin to come alive again. Everything is running smoothly as usual. Daily chores, chapel two times on Sundays and once on Wednesdays and the same sermon: sins of the flesh and honor thy father and mother. Sheet day on Wednesday and again on Saturday, and the week begins again.

It's nine fifty, lights out. With a couple of flickers we have ten minutes to get settled in for the night. There are so many nights I wish I could sit up and listen to my transistor radio and talk or watch a late movie or stay awake. I assume rules are needed when there are fifty girls living under one roof. I doubt if we could get into any more trouble than we are already in right now.

A Night Raid

On a few occasions, bored and way too hungry, we ignore the dangers and raid the kitchen. We tiptoe down the long dark hallway in night-clothes and socks, trying not to laugh. I find a banana and Beth grabs some crackers. Marie and Barbara search the cabinets and under the sinks. After we've pilfered the kitchen and are satisfied with our take, we tuck our findings into the folds of our smocks, holding up the hems like a bowl. We take off on a dead run with high steps on our tiptoes, back up the stairs to the second floor and our room. We don't want to leave any banana peels or crumbs or apple cores as evidence. We sit on our beds, sharing our take and chatting. It's a lot of fun with rich rewards once we are safe. Food is locked up at night, but we have fun breaking in for a midnight snack. The Salvation Army is turning us into thieves. These excursions don't last long; we only attacked the kitchen three times. If caught we might get kicked out, but we have to try.

On one of our late night expeditions, we realize that after "lights out" there is no one here. We are practically alone in this entire building, except for the nurse on the third floor who attends to the babies in the nursery. There must be more adults, but we can't find them, or hear them. The hallways are dark, except for a dim light bulb in the stairwell. You can hear a pin drop. Speaking into the mesh square located next to the delivery room door on the third floor is the only way to receive help. I feel vulnerable, and my sense of security vanishes. Booth Memorial Hospital houses fifty pregnant girls and we are alone, waiting for daylight.

Another prank we did was short sheet beds, when a girl goes to the showers. One girl in particular is Camille. She is blond, quiet and seems confused as to why she is here. She dances with us, but doesn't laugh or get any of our jokes. The first time we short sheet her bed, we wait until she comes out of the showers; Beth and I run back to our room and wait. Camille finally crawls into bed, tries to stretch out, can't, and sleeps in a ball. I felt terrible about that, but we continue to short sheet her bed a few more times. She finally gets the game and laughs a little, showing some humor; it was all in fun. We remake her bed and she begins to open up. Not much, she lacks in the verbal department. She confirms our suspicions; she really has no idea how she landed in a home for unwed mothers.

When we tire of dancing we take turns running and sliding in our socks, not down the main hallway, but the short hallway that connects our rooms to the parlor. To our surprise, Camille was the sliding queen, that girl went all the way to the pillars in the middle of the parlor. We cheered her on, and she seemed happy for the first time.

Morning dawns on a warm August day. My balcony serves me well. I look out toward the bay. My eyes fill with tears. As I blink them away, my smock blows in the morning breeze. On this morning there is news. The story of the death of Marilyn Monroe spreads like wildfire through the home. She committed suicide. I am devastated. I want to be home with my friends and share my grief. Beth walks out to me. She is due any day and can't be bothered with such trivia. She is worried about me and we stand together. She wonders why Marilyn Monroe would kill herself, comments that it's too bad and walks off, her legs apart, her front sticking out farther than mine. The news of her death is all that is on the television and plays over and over. I continue to stare into the distance and grieve over a stranger, a movie star. I had not realized how far away from home I was until this moment. I am not sure if I am crying for Marilyn or for myself.

THE COUNTRY CLUB

Two weeks ago a notice was posted on the events board. The ladies of the Bay Area Country Club are treating us to a day of fun in the sun. Our gift is a buffet and swim party in a private setting. I jump at the chance to swim again. I can imagine the water on my sore back and relish the chance to swim laps again. I turn toward Beth and she shakes her head no, a flat refusal. There is no way she is going to go to a fancy white country club, ride in their cars, line up like a poor pickaninny and eat their food. I try to change her mind, but she keeps to her word and walks away, but not before she issues a word of warning. Barbara is resting her sore back and does not want to go with us either. Five days later the big day arrives, the Country Club outing.

The club women arrive in seven cars, freshly washed and shiny, lined up in the back driveway. It looks like a parade. Marie and I crawl into the back seat of the jet black Buick.

Marie and I are the furthest along in our pregnancy and look forward to this lush setting and the exotic foods. The other girls are new at the home, their bellies not as swollen as ours. Under my floral smock I proudly wear my sister's white one-piece bathing suit. Marie wears a hot pink halter smock. She looks righteous. She resembles a body builder, and her arms with mounds of muscles are toasted from the sun. The Home loaned us towels and we are ready to spend the day baking in the sun and swimming. Marie is Italian and the sun is her best friend. It is hopeless for me with my red hair and freckles. I sport not a wink of color and my long skinny arms dangle at my sides.

The ladies who drive us to the countryside are rich and stuffy and too polite to be real. Their perfume is as stifling as their silence. I prefer to keep a curious eye on the scenery as we zoom up into the green hills of wealth. Then, after one too many hairpin curves, we begin to get car sick. The winding roads are getting worse and we need air. My mouth begins to water so I crack the window and put my face against the narrow burst of cold air. Marie does the same. I can see the line of cars ahead of us. They look like marching ants going up a hill and out of sight, past one curve and then the next.

Our car stops behind the others, and one by one we emerge. I look toward the clubhouse and take notice of faces looking out at us. I suppose a parade of seventeen pregnant teens must have been a sight and worth watching. Beth was right; it is a pity party. We are an oddity.

The ladies are bursting with pride at having rescued us poor pregnant girls. Marie sits on the edge of the pool and dangles her feet. The others carefully begin to pull off their cover-ups and watch. None of us know what to do; there is no instruction or invitation. I go to the edge and don't care who is looking. My smock goes flying through the air and into a chair.

I dip my foot into the cold water, slip my body into the water and take off. I swim five laps before I'm disabled by a leg cramp.

The frog crawl helps get me back to safety at the side of the pool. Hanging on to the edge I walk my hands until I reach the shallow end. I pretend to be in control and relaxed, not wanting to alert the ladies I am in distress. My legs hurt; they feel like they are being squeezed in the roller on our washing machine. I take a deep breath, go under water and massage my cramped muscles. I need to get out of this pool quickly. I look toward Marie who is moving about and freezing. Her lips are blue. We scramble for the towels.

A breeze comes up and the air turns cold. The girls paddle around and seem happy. Another group is hanging on to the edge, moving their legs in a desperate attempt to stay in shape. Few girls go past the shallow end. The water is colder than I remembered from high school. One by one the girls get out and curl up on their towels. Within a short time we are dressed, shivering, and wait to be invited inside.

Then she came around the corner. She is our age, thin, tan and fit, her long blond hair pulled back into a ponytail swinging with each step. She drops her towel to reveal a sparse red bikini. She walks straight to the far end of the pool to the diving board. Slow motion is her game. She walks to the end of the board and begins to bounce like a beach ball. She bounces higher and higher. Then, like an angel from heaven, she does a beautiful swan dive. I feel a welcome perverted happiness as she hits the ice cold water.

The pool party is inside now, and no one is on the patio. She continues to bounce and dive, climb out of the water, squeeze the water from her ponytail and step back onto the diving board. We watch from inside and try to enjoy our luncheon and respond mannerly to the food offerings, pretending not to notice the watchful eyes of the ladies. We try to be calm, stay relaxed and enjoy their efforts. I regret not bringing a sweater. I feel so uncomfortable that I can't bring myself to sit in a chair. I stand next to Marie and we wait. Plates of perfectly sliced vegetables wait for us. I wonder if any of the women take notice of our uncomfortable situation. We patiently wait to be taken back to Booth Memorial.

I feel betrayed. Not one of the seven hosts is conscious enough to ask the young diving princess to take notice and leave. She continues to practice her dives as we nibble on vegetables like fertile pregnant rabbits. It ruins our outing along with whatever self esteem we have left. I think to myself, "It's okay to talk to us, we're not contagious."

Late in the day, just in time for dinner, we arrive back at our safe place. We are all car sick and chilled to the bone. During dinner Beth listens with compassion as I relive our day. She looks back at me with anger in her dark eyes as I vent about the young, sexy, unwelcome guest.

Marie and I are depressed for days. We slop around the halls, flop on to our beds, or stay curled up in a ball after our chores. We have no interest in anything. We go about our daily chores both feeling like fat pregnant pigs. We should have stayed in hiding. Being exposed was a mirror reflecting back to us our shameful existence. Our self-pity journey ends when we notice an empty chair at lunch; Barbara is in labor. Our quiet, nonintrusive friend is now on the third floor.

Beth has left me alone during these dark days. She knows I will come alive in a couple of days, and I do. We take off to the parlor, talk to some of the girls and read magazines. Marie has a more difficult time with depression. We leave her alone until her dark cloud passes.

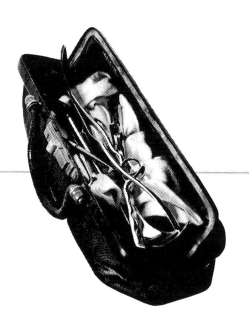

EXAM DAY

Today is Tuesday, scheduled exam day. We scour the list to see if our names and time are listed. My name is not posted this week; Beth's is, so is Marie and Camille. The three of them leave for the third floor and wait next to the wall with the others. One by one the nurse calls the next name. There are no chairs provided.

My first exam went like this. The nurse called my name and I went in. My toe was still in bandages from the mini-surgery. I walked in with my big toe sticking up in the air. She handed me a well-used cotton hospital gown. She told me to put it on, open in the back, and to wait. She ordered me to stand on the scale, then pointed to the examining table. She proceeded to take my blood pressure and put a thermometer under my tongue.

The doctor was behind the curtain with another girl. I heard quiet talking and moving about as she was getting dressed. He washed his hands and came around the curtain to my table. He was younger than

I expected, blond and clean-cut. The door opened, then shut, and the next girl was being weighed and went behind the curtain. A young, handsome doctor only added to my modesty and embarrassment. He told me to scoot down so my bottom was almost off the end. He put my feet into the stirrups, told me to scoot down farther, and to relax. This is the same as telling someone to enjoy the weather as they stand in front of a firing squad.

The doctor said something to the nurse who went into the lab and returned rolling a tray with instruments. This was a bad sign. This was the same feeling I had when I was sitting on the exam table with an ingrown toenail, a bad aura. My heart was in my throat. I turned my head to the side and looked out the window and waited. He used forceps to open me wider and without warning he inserted a needle and gave me a shot. I didn't scream. I gripped the sides of the bed. I could feel the burn; my eyes filled with tears as I squirmed. I don't recall if I made an actual sound or if the moan was in my mind. He placed the needle back on the tray, stood up and left. The nurse also left and I rolled over toward the window and cried. This was my journey into pregnancy and my third day away from home.

Weeks later I stand in line on exam day and visit with the others. I know nothing can ever be as bad as the young doctor with the needle. Even though exam day is routine, we naturally feel apprehensive. Each time it's a different doctor; you never know who you will get. He reads my chart, but says nothing and measures my stomach in both directions. He listens to the heartbeat, never sharing the sound of the tiny beats, and gives no information about my weight or blood pressure. I finally get up the nerve to ask why I am so thin. He blurts out my current weight and continues with the exam. The nurse is finished with my vitals. She takes a razor with a point, holds one finger and pricks the end. She squeezes my finger until a little speck of blood pops to the surface and she wipes the blood onto a glass. This little nip on the end of my finger is the worst and most painful part of the exam. My heart is throbbing at the end of my finger. The throbbing continues throughout the day. You can always tell which girls went upstairs; they are the girls walking around with a bandage on their finger complaining.

On another exam day I went in and waited with apprehension. In walks a handsome colored doctor. He is nicer than the others and the first thing he does is pick up my foot; he looks at my toe and the bandages and remarks that I have pretty feet and unusually high arches. He notices my lack of weight gain and orders a chocolate protein drink. He measures my stomach and listens to its heartbeat and takes my blood pressure. He is nice and gentle. All of the girls hope to get him on exam day; his name is Doctor Copeland.

THE SECRET ROOM

It happened one night. Beth is close to her delivery date and her back aches at night. I am in my eighth month. Our friend Sue lives on the same floor where the delivery room is located. There are three rooms on a wing that juts out from the building. Sue has a secret. She says she and her roommates have watched births. Sometimes the nurses forget to close the window shades and if they're up, you can look across the courtyard toward the window. It's as plain as a large television set. We listen, hungry for details.

It's a hot muggy day. It's been two weeks since the secret room was exposed. Sue's roommate candidly tells us after breakfast that Sue's water broke this morning and she's in labor. The shades are up. We dash up to her room in anticipation to watch Sue's delivery. We look to the left and see the labor room. There she is. Sue stays curled up and hardly moves as the nurse lifts the sheet to check her. This continues for hours. We leave for lunch, do our chores in record-breaking time, then we return. Dinner is over and we go back upstairs, nonchalant so we don't bring attention to our movements. Lights flicker; we have ten minutes to get back to our room and into bed. Beth and I jump into bed with our clothes on. After lights out we count the minutes and then tiptoe back up the stairs with our pillows under our arms to soften our vantage point.

There are seven of us in the bleachers, ready to watch a live birth. One by one girls grow weary and leave. Some sneak back in. We continue to sit in the dark and watch. The theater-goers consist of me, Beth, Sue's three roommates, a new girl from Sausalito, and Marie. We kneel at the windows. Adjustments are needed. We sit on our hips to relieve our knees, but nothing helps ease the hard linoleum floor. We use our pillows as support, our arms rest on the windowsill. We wait and watch with wide innocent eyes.

It seems like an eternity when the huge floodlights click on and the nurses roll the bed with Sue in it. They transfer her to the delivery table. We sit in the dark. They work under floodlights. The shades are up and so is the window. We see Sue's short black hair and listen to her screams. Sue continues to scream and moan; we watch frozen. The nurse puts Sue's legs into the stirrups and straps down her arms. She tries to sit up but is restricted. Over and over she lifts her head, then goes back down. Her legs are apart and we see blood. Beth stands, says she's seen enough, and bolts. I continue to watch, my face frozen to the screen into the window of reality.

More screams as she fights the constraints. Then we see something dark, a round dark thing pushing out from between her thighs. Blood oozes out also. I hear a tribal scream, an animal-like sound, and in seconds a baby is in the arms of the nurse. The room is alive with well rehearsed professionals who care for the infant and Sue. One nurse walks over and pulls down the shade. Movie over.

None of us says a word. We each leave the room with our answer.

How dumb of them to leave a window open. They never knew we watched in darkness. It's late; I sneak back to my room. It's 4:00 A.M.

The next morning Beth and I wake up; she lifts her head and I see her night cap. She looks at me and warns me not to mention the birth. Back down her head goes. I tell her to behave or I'll blurt out the ending. We finally sit up and dangle our legs over the sides of our beds. Tired, the urge to crawl back under the covers is huge.

We notice our swollen kneecaps. They move from side to side and appear to be floating. We hobble downstairs to breakfast and then up to the nurses' station. The nurse gently pushes the puffiness and tells us we have water on the knee. She questions us about why this happened. Stone-faced, we both lie and tell her we were cleaning the floor.

Last night Beth bolted on cue. I waited until the end. Now I am completely scared and my brain goes back to that familiar place called denial. Sue was out of shape and resisted. It can't be that bad. Beth continues to threaten me not to describe one thing.

BETH'S TURN

Beth is uncomfortable, and she is ready for this to be over. I continue to follow her around from place to place. Posted on the bulletin board is the Labor Day party in a week and a half. This is a redundant invitation. They are going to serve ice cream sundaes and serve a meal of hot dogs or hamburgers and soft drinks. I hope Beth is not here for this or she will be pulling her hair out. We roam around and end up in the crafts store. She shows me her creation, the bunny cookie jar. Odd little thing: jacket, big gray ears, kinda scary lookin'.

All I can say to her is, "Nice bunny."

When I first arrived in early June I walked into my room and all I saw were two colored girls and one white girl. I never thought in a million years I would become best friends with a colored girl. I was sheltered from the outside world, living in a small town in central California. My grandma, who is from the South, always told me when I grow up, it is very important to stay within our own race. Now here I am, grieving the potential loss of my roommate, my beautiful, dark-skinned roommate. I love her and cling to her friendship. I love her hair, her smile, and her long dark legs. I look for her when we go our separate ways during the daytime. We both stick together like two flies on a screen door on a hot summer's day.

Beth knows the rules; once you go upstairs, that's it. Your secret is over and you have your life back. She didn't feel good all day; we sit on our beds and groom ourselves as usual. Beth with her lotions, me with my cocoa butter, we rub our swollen bodies like we've done a hundred times. We talk about the possibility of her leaving during the night. She needs sleep; I agree but it's a lie. I hardly sleep a wink all night. I have four more weeks to go and I am frightened to be left alone. I am scared for her. But she is experiencing false labor; this is something new. If we had received information on pregnancy, maybe we would have known.

A week passes before her real labor begins. Sunday morning Beth is up before the chickens. Today is August 19, 1962. She whispers in my ear that this is for real. She packs her small suitcase. I prop up on my elbow, watch and wait. I am sleepy and try to adjust my eyes to the dark. She tells me that this is it; she is heading upstairs. She promises to get in touch with me, or I can come up and see her when I deliver paper products. The early morning has me confused and I am not fully grasping the situation. It's probably another false alarm. I wish her luck, curl up and watch her walk out. She stops, turns around and gives me a wink. I pull my covers up and think about the third floor. I'm next in line. I never told her about the blood.

With Beth gone I climb out of bed and slop down the hallway in my faded pink mumu and terrycloth sandals. Downstairs to the basement toward the dining room I go. It's Sunday of all days. I have to spend the day alone, look at her empty chair, and attend chapel, twice. The Salvation Army is pounding Christianity into our heads. They remind us three times a week of our sinful ways, sinful deeds, and the wrath of God we have inflicted on ourselves and our parents. Repent, you naughty girl, the constant reminder of our wanton ways. I wish I could stand up just once and say, "Stop, let's talk about something else; there must be more to the *Bible* than just sin." But I sit in silence on my sore tailbone and sing with my sinful voice, kneel on my boney sinful knees, pray with my sinful mind, then exit through the heavy door with the stained glass.

ALONE

I can't take it anymore. It has been a week since I last saw Beth, standing in our doorway. With a wink she was gone; I am as low as I can get. Down the concrete steps I walk, straight downhill four blocks toward our little store with the saggy awnings. I walk past the store and keep going. Our weekly outings to the market are a faded memory. I think of the girls and keep walking, toward the sun. I continue down the street toward unknown territory. Slowly and without purpose I walk and remember my friends, the first day I arrived, my sweet Uncle Bill, the chocolates, Beth, the pending divorce of my parents. I keep going, wanting to get as far away as I can.

I pass tall buildings, some with kids playing on the steps. I pass cyclone fences with weeds and dogs inside barking. I step on weeds coming up from the cracks. I see old stores closed for good. I am unaware of any danger as I walk away from a nightmare. Cars whiz by as I walk along this long busy street toward freedom. I am due in two weeks. Houses are more run down and businesses begin to roll down awnings and wire security screens. I pass industrial buildings and motor shops. I keep going.

I see a sea of steel strips in the far distance, glints reflecting the sun's rays. There are too many train tracks to count. I walk and wonder if I can get across without being hit by a slow moving train. I am tired and walk slower; my groin is hurting. I place my hand on the bottom of my stomach for support and step onto the tracks. I hear engines, see nothing moving, and keep going.

I know I have walked too far and I'm in pain. I need a restroom but still have many tracks to cross. Across the street is a Sears store and a bench on the side. I keep my focus on the bench and continue to walk. Finally, I am at the light and wait. I go to the other side of the busy street and into the store. I ask directions to the ladies room and re-lieve myself. Back through the racks of clothes I find the double doors and the bench. Relieved, I sit down next to some folks waiting for a bus, take a deep breath and put my head back. I find my composure and notice the buildings are peach-colored. The sun is setting. Cars race by; so do taxi's and trucks. I am in the heart of town at a busy in-tersection. I hear a highway behind us. I have walked five miles. I could have sat there for hours and rested, but I need to get going so I can beat the dark.

I head back across the busy street, the dozens of tracks, following my footsteps down the sidewalks past the tall buildings and dogs barking. I stay the course and go straight back the way I came. By the time I get to the saggy awnings I am in disturbing discomfort. My feet are swollen and my shoes are tight and painful. I am not sure what hurts the most. I turn the corner and head up the hills of tidy houses toward the Home. I trudge along as the hills are steep; only three blocks to go. I wonder if anyone looks out their window and sees us girls. I am invisible as I walk along in discomfort. I make it to the bottom of the steps, look up and sigh. One foot in front of the other is the only way I am going to make it. The sun has set and the steps are difficult to see. I hold on to the handrail and make my way to the front doors.

The front desk is closed. The halls are empty. I head downstairs to the dining room for some food. The girls see me and we get a plate together. I sit and tell them I took off and walked as far as I was able. I gulp water and stare. No one says much to this crazy person who just ran away from, and then returned to a home for unwed mothers. I head upstairs to my room, flop down and sleep all night in my mumu, my dirty swollen feet hanging off the end of my bed.

LABOR DAY PARTY

The Labor Day Party is this weekend. I walk across the driveway where we used to play hopscotch, toward the shade of a huge protective tree. The volunteers put together a hot dog, grab a soda out of an ice bucket and pile on some chips. I eat alone as I do most days now. Eating alone is my choice. There is no need to interact and make friends I will never see again. On the other hand, none of the new arrivals interact with girls ready to deliver; we are too close to reality. My friends are gone; Beth has been gone for two weeks.

I was not able to make contact with Beth again. Marie delivered her baby soon after Beth. I sit here under the shade of the tree eating my lunch and remember Gayle, my first roommate who was always crocheting and happy as a lark, and spunky Nancy who shared with us her zest for life. The cheerleaders from the third floor, the lawyer's daughter, the secretary carrying her boss's child; they have returned to their lives. One girl remains. She is thirteen years old with long, brown, curly hair. She looks Jewish, and the rumor is she is a victim of rape. She has never spoken to anyone to my knowledge and continues to be alone and stone-faced.

No one dances; the Home has a different atmosphere. Maybe it's me; I have become the girl I met when I first arrived. That girl wouldn't talk and was depressed; maybe that's me. The new arrivals tend to stick together for confidence and support. They walk through the same emotional doors we did. I am lonely, but I know my time is near; soon I'll be home.

I have not seen or heard from any of my friends since they each went upstairs. Out of curiosity, I ask around and only one person helps me with my concerns. It is Mrs. Black, one of the nurses. She told me Marie delivered early and let her baby go. Barbara kept her baby; Beth had a baby girl and let her go. I tried in vain to see Beth when she was upstairs; she was locked up tighter than Fort Knox. When I heard the news about my friends keeping their babies I felt happy for them and sad for Beth and Marie. I wrote to Joanie how difficult it is going to be to leave my baby here. This decision and journey are much more difficult than I expected.

The staff asks me to organize the makings of the ice cream sundaes. I think they want to keep me busy. I am bossy as I get bigger and I am the largest girl here. My stomach is sticking out so far I can't see my mother line or my feet. My groin feels like it is going to break into two pieces. One by one we put on the three different flavors. It becomes an assembly line, and I am consumed with efficiency and balance. The day seems to never end. It is a welcome sight when the sun begins to set behind the tall stone building. Beth's image comes into my mind, my beautiful roommate and friend. I have pressure in my groin and tightening stomach muscles, same as she experienced. Room 4 waits. I curl up under the covers in my bed. This is my private time to caress my baby.

Last night many of the girls showered early because tomorrow is the first day of school. I am a junior. Classes begin at 8:00. We rise at 6:30 as usual, go to the dining room, pray, eat. The school is located on the same floor as my room at the opposite end. I'm taking history, English, typing, and bookkeeping. I have twenty days left. There are nine girls in my class and we study many subjects in one room with the same teacher. I love the small classroom and the attention. The teacher can focus on each student and with this special one-on-one attention, I understand and am interested in everything. No distractions. I finish the homework assignments on time without any problems. The classroom is sparse, with windows overlooking a lush landscape. It's a welcome change of scenery. Each student stays focused.

My sister left a message for me to phone home. Today is September 10th. I walk into the office and call home, collect. Bobbie informs me that Grandma and Mother want me to keep my baby. Grandma says our family blood runs through its veins and the baby needs to come home with me. I am shocked and ask her if she is sure. She goes on to say she will paint a dresser and get a crib and baby clothes, and she will help me. Mother will stay home with the baby while I attend school. She says Mother has moved to a town thirty miles away and has rented a two bedroom house and waits for me and my baby. I am still shocked and try to grasp this change of heart. She doesn't mention our father and I wonder if he is part of this plan, or is left out of the blood-in-our-veins loop. She tells me to pick out some names and if it is a boy to name it Robert after her boyfriend. I go back to my room and lie on my bed with my stationery and begin to write down names for a boy and a girl.

The shocking change of heart brings joy and added stress. I will be facing my lies head-on, and I will have an illegitimate baby. The town might turn against me. One of my uncles has already warned me not to bring a bastard child into our family. If this is the flavor or my return, I can only survive with the support of my family and friends.

I don't want anyone to be mean to my baby. I guess I have to grow a backbone and face the truth, with my baby in my arms. I need peace and quiet and I need to prepare. I need to circle the wagons and get my friends to support my decision. Oh how I wish Joanie was here to help me. My situation has gone from shock, to confinement, to a full blown soap opera.

I have a sinking feeling in my gut that my father is not aware of the change of plans. I bet this is my sister's idea. I know my mother will be happy and grandma too.

My uncle will be apologetic someday; my father will go bananas.

This is complicated. I don't know what last name to put on the birth certificate.

MY TURN ON THE THIRD FLOOR

Today is September 14th, a Friday. I don't feel good. I'm tired and have a lower back ache. I shower, lotion my body and go to bed directly after dinner. Now it's 1:00 A.M. I have been in bed all night timing my contractions; they're every four minutes. I'm under the covers with my portable alarm clock; it has a face and hands that light up green. I decide that it is my turn on the third floor. I get up and retrieve my oversized suitcase and begin to pack. No one wakes up or makes a sound. I walk out of Room 4 for the last time and never look back. I step into the dark hallway and reach the staircase to begin my climb. Each step takes all of my will and strength. I inch my body up one or two steps, then have to stop and rest. Sometimes I make it three steps before another contraction hits. I lug my suitcase, sit down with my arms over the top, and hang on to the handle. The pains are worse as time ticks by; no one is awake and there is no sound on the second floor.

Two more steps and I have to sit down again and put my head on my suitcase and wait for the pain to go away. There is one small dingy yellow light bulb in the stairwell. It's so faint I can barely see my hands in front of me. The stairwell is too dim to see the steps. I inch my way up; my ascent is slow and careful. I use my toes to kick the next step and guide me upward to the landing. I hang onto the rail and feel my way with each foot. I take a step, drag my suitcase and continue to put it down and collapse. Once again my head goes down to the suitcase, and my hands cluth the handle. I hold my breath and wait it out. Another pain. I am now beginning to feel scared, not of having a baby, but of falling and breaking my neck. I have four minutes to move upward toward the top of this never ending dark staircase. I assume I have four minutes between contractions; my clock is in my suitcase. I'm guessing because it's too dark to see my wristwatch. This dark journey consists of one or two stairs at a time; me dragging my suitcase, sitting, waiting as I continue to move closer to the dreaded third floor. With a push I try to get my suitcase to move with me. I tell myself, "just another few steps." This scene repeats for two hours. I'm worried and scared of the dark. One step then the next. I don't want to deliver my baby on a stairwell but the night is closing in. I finally make it to the third floor, lug my cumbersome stupid suitcase down the hall until I see the gold mesh square screen. Tonight for the first time I speak into it and say, "This is Judi G. I am in labor." I slump over my suitcase, take a deep breath and wait. The wide white door opens.

The nurse comes out with a wheelchair and shoves my suitcase into the room. I am put on the bed next to the window and have two more contractions. My lower back is hurting and so is the lower part of my stomach, and to my surprise, my thighs even hurt. The night nurse checks my temperature and takes my blood pressure. She tells me to undress and put on a soft cloth hospital gown. In between dressing the pains continue. She asks me when the contractions began and I said, "About 9:00 P.M. and I came up at 1:00 A.M." She tells me that it's 3:00 A.M., and asks what I have been doing for the last two hours. I curl up with another pain and tell her I have been on my hands and knees in the stairwell or sitting on my suitcase. She puts on gloves and pours something on her hand and checks me. It is 3:30 A.M. Saturday morning, sheet day. I wonder if Beth was in this same bed and all the others before me.

The nurses change shifts at 6:00 A.M. The morning nurse walks in and it's Mrs. Black. She is pretty, a sweet colored nurse who knows how to make you feel loved. She cares and is much more tender than the last nurse. She takes my temperature and blood pressure again and puts on her rubber gloves with the same liquid and checks me, same as the nurse before did so many times I lost count. She looks worried; I am hurting and have to go to the bathroom. She helps me stand and helps guide me, holds me up until I can hang onto the wall. Mrs. Black goes to the phone and makes a call. I go to back to bed and continue to labor and wait. Mrs. Black brings me juice and a piece of toast. I continue with my contractions. Mrs. Black tells me she called the doctor; she is concerned about something. It's Saturday noon.

Turns out I'm allergic to the liquid the nurses have put on their gloves every time they checked me. I have had a reaction and swelling. Soon three other doctors arrive. I can hear them conferring; all three doctors stand over me and watch me whither in pain as they discuss my swollen privates. Dr. Copeland is one of these doctors. He puts on a glove with nothing on it and checks me to see if I am able to deliver a baby. I am so swollen it appears I have grown testicles. My father will finally get the son he's always wanted. I'm not scared because I am in too much discomfort to worry about my bottom, and I don't understand what is happening, the seriousness of my condition. I concentrate and focus on my pains and on the tender raw area created by the liquid flesh eating gel. It's a huge relief when the nurses discontinue the exams. I am uncomfortable to say the least, and the swelling is getting worse.

The doctors leave and the nurse comes in and tells me to take a cool shower. She hands me a cup and instructs me to splash myself between my legs with cold water and try to cool down the inflammation; do this many times. I had to laugh at the word inflammation. I can feel the swelling dangling between my legs and she refers to it as inflammation. I know I am in big trouble.

The cup of cold water is the best feeling ever. I begin to toss this magnificent water between my legs when another pain starts in my lower back, comes around to the front of my lower stomach, and my stomach gets as hard as a rock. The shower wall serves as a support for my arms. I put both hands on the white tiles, drop my head and wait. The only thing I know to do for relief is to take a deep breath and hold it until the pain subsides. I add warmer water to the shower and put my head under the nozzle. The water soothes me and relaxes my body; I could stay in here forever. It's a relief to get the disinfectant liquid rinsed off of my privates. A soft towel waits for me outside the stall; I dry off my body and wrap it around my hair. Mrs. Black gently helps me put my arms back into the gown. The shower restores my composure and I get back into bed. It's a bed with fresh sheets and I didn't have to make it. They re-hook me to the IV with two bags of liquid that drop into two separate needles, one taped to the inside of my arm and the other one stuck into the top of my hand. No one checks me the rest of the day. My chart must have read, "Stay clear of Judi's privates."

My labor is intense and the clock continues to tick. Mrs. Black puts a pillow under my back and turns me to my side. Labor is more painful than I expected, more intense. I had no idea and I don't have much time to breathe between pains. I have a pillow between my knees and that helps with the pressure on my lower back. The pains come and go and I rest. Mrs. Black brings in a wet wash cloth and wets my lips. She checks my temperature, blood pressure, but does not go near my privates. The swelling between my legs begins to subside. It took three doctors to concur that the best solution was a cool shower splash. I continue to curl up and wait. When I have a pain I hold my breath and keep quiet. The night closes in and the sun comes up, and Mrs. Black is back on shift. Sunday goes by and still no baby.

Today is Monday. I'm still in labor and seeing Mrs. Black walk toward me is a blessing. I'm pleased to see her. I have been in labor for sixty hours. My pains are one minute apart, sometimes closer. Mrs. Black exclaims, "You still here?"

She teases me and cares for me at the same time. She fluffs my pillows, smoothes the sheets, lifts my head and gives me sips of juice. She checks the needles in my arm and hand and checks my vitals. She then puts some clear gel on her glove and checks me. It must be Vaseline. She asks me if today is the day I'm goin' to have this baby, and I answer in a faint voice, "Yes."

She asks me, "Miss Judi, what time do you think it's goin' t' happen?"

I blurt out, "2:08." She laughs and says she'll hold me to it. I continue to labor.

It's before noon when she comes in with a letter. The letter is from Joanie. Between pains I tear it open. Her first written words to me are, "My dearest Judi, are you in labor yet?"

Thank God someone from home is worried. In between pains I hold the letter tight to my chest, then take a deep breath and reach for the side of the bed and hold tight. I hold on to the bed with one hand, and with the other hand I hold Joanie's letter crinkled to my chest. I'm unable to read another word, but her opening line is enough encouragement for me to continue with my labor. I am more focused and centered. I have another intense pain and think of Joanie; if only you knew. My pains are closer together; I try to breathe and not cry out. I don't want anyone to say I told you so. I keep quiet.

My bottom is shrinking and the nurses begin to check me with a dab of Vaseline, or something less flesh-eating. Mrs. Black says I'm coming along. The pains are more intense. I guess I am supposed to know what the term "coming along" means. I curl up in a ball and wait and continue to hold my breath with each pain. The letter is still in my hand. It's 1:30 P.M. and the nurse checks me often. I don't flinch, nor do I care what they see or do to me.

My body decides to go into a sky dive; I didn't know what pain was up until this point. I have no idea what happens to Joanie's letter. The memory of this moment is the sound of wheels; my bed wheels: the curtain wheels, the bright light on wheels, lots of rolling sounds. I hear Mrs. Black talking to someone and I feel my bed begin to roll into the delivery room, which is actually the same room separated by a curtain.

The lights are blinding bright; Mrs. Black and another nurse transfer my body to the delivery table. They must be crazy if they think I am going to let go of these bed rails, but I do. Somehow I get onto the delivery table and there is continuous movement all around me, a commotion. I'm thankful Mrs. Black is with me, then I see Dr. Copeland. The other nurse puts my feet onto the cold silver stirrups and straps my ankles while the nurses talk among themselves. They take hold of my arms and strap each arm down to the sides of the bed. Now I am strapped down unable to move my arms when someone puts a lever into each hand. My legs are in a bent position and I am in extreme pain. The pain has decided to go into my lower back, come around to the front and hit head on full force like two rams fighting. Dr. Copeland sits down on a stool between my legs and begins once again talking about my high arches.

He says," Mrs. Black, look at this girl's arches, I have never seen arches so high." She looks at my feet and nods in agreement that indeed I do have high arches. I feel another pain and try not to arch my feet so Dr. Copeland will pay attention to the main event. He paints cold orange liquid on my inner thighs and I feel my water break, hot liquid coming out of me. I have pains that make me want to push; the lights are in my face and on my private area. Don't arch your feet Judi. Whatever you do, don't arch. A sweet nurse rubs my arms and my doctor is focused on something. I have the urge to push again and they tell me to pull up with the levers in my hands, pull and push at the same time. I bear down, pull up and push harder. I do this for a long time, my skin tearing as the baby moves closer. I continue to push and push again, when I feel pressure and then this total and superior relief. I push again, then feel something slip out from inside of me. At the same time my stomach goes concave. An ultimate warm feeling comes over me. In an instant the pain is gone and I hear a baby cry. The baby is taken away, and the nurses tend to its needs. The doctor finishes with the delivery, retrieving the after birth, and he begins to stitch me up. Darn it, I didn't want to tear. While he is stitching I can feel the needle; my bottom is not numb. This is very painful, almost as much as the delivery.

Mrs. Black walks over to my head, bends down to my ear and in a sweet voice says, "Judi, look back behind you to the clock."

I arch my neck, look to the wall behind me and see a huge round clock. It's 2:08.

I have a son.

Doctor Copeland continues to stitch up the tear and asks me if I have learned my lesson. I quickly think about this question and if I say no, he might sew me shut for life, so I answer, "Yes Sir." He is pleased with my answer and continues. I'm tired and happy and scared. I was in labor for sixty five hours.

I am wheeled into the mothers' quarters. I wake up to shooting pains between my legs. My stitches are screaming and I need medication. I decide that the squeaky wheel gets oil so I call out for a nurse. This continues for my full seven-day stay and I am sure they will tell me goodbye and whisper, good riddance.

The care in the mothers' quarters is excellent. I guess they want our last memory to be a good one. The walls are light yellow, the beds soft and comfortable. The nurses are attentive and help us care for our babies when we are too tired. We are the lucky ones keeping our babies. The birth mothers who are not keeping their babies are coached not to hold them; some do, others don't. I get up at feeding time, sit on a pillow and rock and feed my son. I complain and get medication for my stitches. The food is better than I have had all summer. I rest and enjoy sleeping on my stomach during my seven day stay. I try to be cheerful, but I am beaten down emotionally. I am anxious to see my mother. My mother and sister will be here on Monday. I look forward to our reunion and our exit .

I'm anxious to go home, but our home has been sold, our furniture auctioned off, and how do I explain a baby? Joanie will be exposed for all of the stories and excuses she made up. I need to focus and not dwell on the dark stuff.

HOME WITH MY SON

It is a long drive home. My sister stops a couple of times for us to stretch and tend to the baby's needs. Driving down the Central Valley is like sticking a needle in your eye over and over again. There is nothing to do except bounce in our small car in heavy traffic, listening to the hum of the engine and watching the tall rows of oleander bushes standing in an endless line on either side of the highway. In the back seat, I sit on a pillow while my son sleeps.

We talk about the future and the baby and what to say and how to handle the situation. Mother is quiet and we listen to Bobbie, who is once again full of ideas. Finally, after taking a long bumpy ride of five hours, we reach my mother's new home, a tiny house located in Exeter, thirty miles from my hometown. I am home but still in hiding. We decide that if anyone asks, the baby belongs to my sister. Bobbie helps us unload the car, then goes home to be with her little girl Tammy, who is 18 months old. Bobbie's day begins at 5:00 A.M.

I go into my new bedroom. There is a nicely made twin bed, a table with a lamp and a new dress set out for my first day of school. I slip it on. It has brown and black swirls with a pleated skirt of light material and fits perfectly. I lie down in my new dress and begin to weep and then cry uncontrollably. I cry until my sobs turn into sucking air. I feel mother's soft hands rubbing my legs and the back of my new dress. It only makes me cry harder.

She gives up and goes into the kitchen. I hear her heating up the milk to feed my son. The sound plunges me deeper into hysterics. I am tired, my stitches burn, my breasts are swollen with milk and I am out of control. The room is dark. Only a beam of light comes from the living room down the short hallway. Slowly I pull up onto my elbows to sit on the edge of the bed in my new dress with my legs dangling off, my hair standing on end. I wonder what has become of me.

I go into the front room to help. My baby is asleep in his grandma's arms. I take my son away from her and begin to rock him back and forth while Mother has a chance to shower and relax. The motion of rocking helps me get centered and regain my composure. After a while Mother begins to fix us something to eat, and later she comes out of the kitchen with two bowls of ice cream. She is also tired from the long drive, but helps any way she can. Mother is tiny with short black hair and brown eyes. We look nothing alike, not in body or coloring. Yet I have the same expressions and I also like to look after friends and little ones with compassion. We work well together.

We take turns with feedings every four hours, sometimes every two hours. He has his days and nights mixed up and that is not fun for us, but he seems happy. We take turns bathing him in the kitchen sink, wrap him in a towel, then douse him with baby powder. I nickname him Chuck from his name Robert Charles. He has blondish-red hair and very long arms and legs; he resembles my father and Tom. I also resemble my father. Somewhere in there is me.

Today I have to rise early and go to Exeter High school and enroll. I attended grade school here in second, third and fourth grades, then again in sixth grade. I might know some of the kids. We kept moving back and forth for my father's work.

Early mornings I feed my son and change his clothes and lay him in the living room in his bassinette. I then yank the rollers out of my hair, backcomb it to a nice big bubble and slip into my new dress. Life goes on, but this time life is going on with the addition of sleepless nights and homework. Tomorrow is picture day.

Mother cares for my son while I attend school. I walk home and rock him, feed him and read my books; I sit in the bathtub in shallow hot water to help heal my stitches. I am a junior in high school by day, sharing my lunch table and getting reacquainted with old grade school friends, and by night I am feeding my baby and soaking my stitches.

It has been two weeks of this intense schedule and today is my six-teenth birthday. Mother bakes a cake and friends from Porterville drive over and bring baby gifts. Dennis stops by and so does Rita my sweet friend who never asks any questions. I make eye contact with her and she says, "Poor Nana," her nickname for me.

They don't stay long. Uncomfortable situation I suppose. Mother suggests she take a photo of me holding my son on this special day. She suggests we go to the back of the house in case anyone drives by and sees me holding a baby. Still hiding, I follow my mother and the camera. I squat and caress my baby in my arms and look up at the camera with a big smile. Mother takes another photo of me looking down at him and another of me feeding him, all in the privacy of our backyard. These photos are priceless, and they will be the only pictures of me with my son.

Two weeks after my sixteenth birthday I walk home from school as usual. The house is eerily quiet. I tip-toe into mother's bedroom and I see my baby sound asleep in his bassinet. I look at Mother and she returns my gaze with pleading eyes. Her face is sagging on one side and she cannot move. I run to the phone and dial my sister, "I think Mother has had a stroke." I go back to Mother and take her hand in mine and gently touch her face. I tell her that help is on the way. Within thirty minutes, which is how long it takes to drive from our hometown, my sister arrives as does my father.

My father has been a ghost in this family. He keeps his distance so he won't tarnish his good name. This phase of my life is a blur; I have no concept of what happens or the steps taken to care for my mother who has indeed suffered a massive stroke. I have no memory of moving back to Porterville, her medical care or changing schools, nor do I know if I attended school right away. I have no recall of who is even caring for my son.

I do remember while I waited for help to arrive that my son began to fuss and squirm, this I do remember. I changed him, heated a bottle, fed him, burped him, and with the baby in my arms, I sat on the side of the bed next to mother and waited. I disassociate from my mother's suffering and tend to my baby instead. The rest of the room is a blur of my sister, my father and other people beginning to mill about. Then I shut down.

My next memory is of us living back in Porterville. Mother is recovering and I'm enrolled into my old high school. It's almost November and approximately three weeks since we left Exeter. I have been a junior for two months and this is my third high school.

Mother and I continue our daily routine, me in school and she caring for my son as best she can. My cousin's wife Nancy is over a lot to help with the baby, and after work my sister stops in the afternoons with little Tammy. My dad is estranged from us, living across town. But he somehow keeps a watchful eye on our daily activities and finances. All other relatives stay clear of us; we are a family in crisis and this could be contagious.

It is now November. I am still thin, weak and depressed. I try to blend in at school and smile, but I am not the same person. I once carried my books and a small black wallet; now I have more baggage than a department store warehouse. I lug my summer memories around with me like a bag like full of freshly picked cotton. I miss Beth and think of her often and vow to find her one day.

Then it all comes crashing down. Without warning I contract the Asian flu and strep throat. I am in bed for a week with a fever that spikes 105. I have stomach cramps and a raw throat and my baby cries to be fed, changed and held. I have no idea who's helping me, mother and Nancy I assume. Sister Bobbie stays away to not get contaminated. I hope my dad contacted the school about my absence.

It is about the sixth day of fever and chills when I become aware of my mother, who has crept into my room and places the baby in his crib. She comes back over to me and gently lays a cool cloth on my forehead. She sits beside me and tells me the news. Nancy, my cousin's wife who is always lurking about, has relatives in Fresno; they have a small farm and a country store. They are unable to have children and want very much to adopt my son. I lie there curled up in a ball and listen. She goes on to say that the baby would have a father and a good home. I listen. I roll over and shiver, pull the blankets higher. The fever is in control of my body and I am chilled to the bone. I close my eyes and will myself to be strong and healthy.

A few days later I am aware of mother sitting next to me. She tells me the family will be here in an hour to take the baby. I have no idea who the mastermind is behind this plan. I have my suspicions and they are the ones who will have to live with this busybody interaction for the rest of their lives. I lie there and wait. Finally I get up and hold my son. With him in my arms, I sit on the edge of the bed and look at his face. He's beginning to fill out. I try to imagine him as a grown man. I will myself to sear his face into my mind and never forget. I undo the baby blanket and look at his long legs and arms and hold his feet in my hands. I whisper to him I'm sorry. I sit and hold him and feel the warmth of his body next to me. I know what little time I have left with him is growing near.

I want him to have a good life, a life on a farm with a mother and a father and security, which seems to be out of reach for me. Mother says they already have adopted a little girl who is three years old; he will grow up with a big sister.

They're here. I hear two car doors slam shut. I throw on a sweater and baggy pants and make my way into the living room. The scene is quiet, uncomfortable and oddly out of step. I put the baby in my mother's arms. I listen to the legal woman who takes over and who is definitely in charge of the situation. I take a visual inventory. The man and woman who want my son are both short. She is plump, with soft dark curls and sprinkles of gray, and she wears glasses. He has a slight build, thinning light blond hair; they both seem nervous, but nice and polite. They also look like country folk, which reminds me of my grandma whom I adore. They look to be approximately 60 years old, but they are in their early 40s.

My sister, Mother and I sit on the couch. I become deaf. I only hear the sounds of a freight train in my head, drowning out the words everyone speaks as though I'm not here. I notice a little girl standing in the corner by the front door, a girl with short dark straight hair and straight across bangs. She looks at me. I stare back at her. This will be my son's big sister. This encounter, this still frame moment of me and a little girl looking at each other is the only peace and comfort I have.

Finally the time comes. Mother begins to hand the baby into the waiting arms of the nameless new mother. I swallow, sit up and begin to listen. The legal woman motions mother to wait, saying, "This is only legal if Judi holds the baby and places the baby into the new mother's arms." This is a brutal and barbaric idea and it's not fair. I loathe this woman for making me do such a thing. For once I speak out. I stand up and face all the adults. I say, "I promise you I will not make any trouble, and promise I will not attempt to find him until he is eighteen, and after his eighteenth birthday I will look for him."

I had prepared a baby book soon after we arrived home from Oakland. I carefully glued in the black and white photos of me on my sixteenth birthday, holding him and smiling. I wrote down the history of his real parents, his grandparents and great grandparents, on both sides of our families. The book is white silk with blue flowers.

The new mother stands to get the baby. She reaches out and I hand her the baby book instead. I ask both of them to please show him this book when he is older. Everyone watches our transaction; you could hear a pin drop. She reaches again for my son, but I am not finished yet. I stand in the middle of our living room in full sight, kiss him on top of his head, smell his scent, rub my cheek on his cheek as he sleeps, unaware he is changing mothers; then I look at his face for the last time. I gently place my son into her waiting arms. It is surreal, slow motion. My sister has the clarity to jot down the formula we give him, Similac with iron. I sign papers; they stand to leave. There is no hand shaking. It is a complete and legal agreement, a cold and unfeeling transaction. Today is November 9, 1962.

Mother continues to cook and care for me and the household. My sister stays away as I try to heal from the flu and from the trauma of letting my son go. Bobbie sat with us for the relinquishment, and I'm glad she was there.

I finally get the gumption to call Joanie. She drives over after dinner. She pulls up in front of the house, and I hear a faint knock on the front door. I grab my jacket and we head outside. In the moonlight, in the shadow of our big tree sits her dad's pink Edsel. We climb in and sit. Taking deep breaths, we both stare at the street ahead. Joanie is gentle with me and listens to what I have to say, which is brief and to the point. I feel numb, confused and guilt-ridden. I tell her I've lost myself, my son and my joy. She's very sorry. She's quiet, and this is what I cherish about her.

"I am here if you need anything," she softly says.

I go on to tell her there is nothing she can do. "This is the darkest day of my life; just be here for me." I tell her that I'm not mad at anyone, only myself. I have no idea who masterminded this plan. I have my ideas, but it was all done in good faith, I hope. I need time to absorb what has happened.

We are together again, but it's not the same. We're quiet; she tells me about her family and their drama and I listen closely. Her story is closely linked to mine. We don't cry. Numb souls don't cry. We don't play music. Bruised spirits don't sing. We don't drink cokes with peanuts, no laughter and no gossip. We just sit and stare.

Finally, she starts the engine and drives us about a mile to Scenic Heights. We call this section of town Pill Hill. This is the only hill in our town and all of the doctors live up here. We wind our way up the road lined with spacious homes. She parks at the turn-around and we just sit and stare, mumble profound statements. We see nothing, hear nothing. We are two friends parked on Scenic Heights at night in a pink Edsel. How pathetic.

It seems like many years since we two girlfriends walked together through the doorway of adulthood. Joanie patiently waits for her next cue, but we're frozen by reality. I tell her that somewhere inside this shell of a person is me, but I can't find me. Where did I go?

I promise her that I'll wait to heal and get my strength back. I'll continue on the journey of life. And mark my words, I will find my son. We sit and watch the lights. We roll down the windows and let the chilly night engulf us, and we wait for an emotion. She turns on the heater, our feet become warm, our arms and faces cold. Here we sit, parked on a hill-top, looking out into the darkness at our hometown. It twinkles like a fairy-tale, but it's not.

PART TWO

MY SON

I kept my promise and searched for my son, and found him when he was 22 years old. The search was a time-consuming, emotional journey. I was shocked when I eventually found him in Arkansas. He stands tall at 6'5"with reddish-blonde hair, brown eyes and a dimple in his chin. He favors Tom and also my father, the two men in his life who were turned upside down by his tiny existence. His new name is David Charles. I was pleased they kept his middle name, after my father.

When I first found him with the help and guidance of ALMA (Adoptive Liberty Movement Association), I phoned him person to person. Naturally, he was caught off guard. I introduced myself as his biological mother, and I heard a young man's voice reply, "Oh my." I told him I was young, I had no choice in the adoption, and I am sorry. I continued on and told him I was on the high school swim team and swam in many events, unaware I was carrying a child. He returned my phone call a few hours later and asked one question, "Did we win?"

His next question was; "What color are your eyes?"

He is lean and as country as you can get. Genetics are powerful. He is much like my other kids. He has a quick wit and comic timing. He can keep an audience in stitches.

I located David in 1984 and within two months he hopped a plane. We met at the Sacramento airport. He lived with us for four months. This was a dream come true and seemed like a good idea. I didn't take into consideration the ramifications of a new addition to our family. Jeff was 15, Dana 10, and Spencer 8. I pushed my husband to the back burner. Soon there was trouble on the horizon.

My oldest son Jeff didn't enjoy having an older brother as much as he'd hoped. He felt dethroned. He wasn't high man on top of the heap, David was. Jeff reacted to David in a negative way. David's life style and my over the top attentiveness compounded Jeff's attitude. David was raised with very little and didn't want Jeff to even sit on his bed. They had words which resulted in confrontation. I had two related alpha males in a parallel position.

I continued to dote on my newfound son. My two older sons tried to connect. David took Jeff fishing on the Sacramento River and they talked late into the night. All the kids swam and played in our pool and watched TV, but it was not smooth sailing. I'd listen to Jeff, and then talk to David about sharing and brotherly love to try and smooth things over. These brothers needed time, time to get acquainted and time to gather shared memories, time they didn't have. David left after 4 months and moved to New Mexico, then to Texas and didn't return for many years. This time his exit was more painful than when he was an infant. I walked into the house, got into the shower and cried until the water ran cold and I was on my knees.

David continues to live in a small town in Arkansas. His passion is cooking. He's built barns, fences and condos. He's also a welder. He's fathered four children and doesn't have contact with any of them. He has logical reasons why, but the bottom line is, he's disconnected. He trusts only a few select childhood friends. He is a likable guy, but unable to establish a long-lasting relationship with a woman. He loves them and leaves them. If the word marriage is mentioned, he's gone into the night.

I feel responsible, but I'm not the one who raised him. He carries different values and morals than the children I raised. He's a sweetheart, but he is not a responsible man as far as money and motivation. He likes to live on the boundaries of poverty. If you are broke, you can't possibly raise a family. I sometimes wonder if he is unwilling to be in a relationship due to changing mothers at age 9 weeks.

The family who stepped into our home that November day in 1962 did not present themselves in a truthful manner. On the adoption papers they lied and stated they were my third cousins. They each wrote they had college educations. The truth is, we are not related; their education stopped at eighth grade. The adoptive mother's maiden name is on the birth certificate as their last name. My name, which was originally on the birth certificate, is erased off the face of the earth. If you conduct a search through microfilm in the same county of your child's birth, the birth certificate states the biological mother's maiden name. Not so in my case. I found him by fierce determination and digging.

David's adoptive parents each had a drinking problem and both were heavy smokers. His adoptive father was not only an alcoholic, but went into drunken rages, and beat his wife while the two little ones hid in the closet. David told me that many times they were also in harm's way and were often the brunt of his anger. They lived below the poverty level on government assistance and his adoptive father had money from being a veteran. They did manage to raise a big strong healthy boy. David relives walking home from school and smelling fresh baked bread coming from his home. If he was living with me he would have smelled my mother's fried chicken and a fresh cut lawn. He has only good things to say about his mother and the daily banter they exchanged. She enjoyed raising him and his humor. Her death spun him into a tailspin of depression.

Irene, his mother, wrote me a letter stating, "We are both in love with the same man, and we both will learn to share and work through this transition." I appreciated her letter and understood. I am blessed to have found him, to be able to hold his large weathered hands in mine, look into his eyes and his mature face and see the lines of life across his brow. I listen to tales about his young life and I am spellbound.

There are many birth mothers who cannot find the babies they were forced to relinquish, and there are biological fathers who are left out of the loop, with no information to search and find their child. Some bio fathers are asked to stay in the shadows and never come forward. The fantasy of finding your child is not always what you dream, but it's a journey that pulls you toward a natural connection.

I've learned the broken bond can never heal. The missing link cannot be replaced. David and I love each other. We have softness toward each other and an awkward bond, but not the same comfortable bond he feels for the mother who raised him.

I have also learned that genetics play a huge role in personality. He was voted most fun of his senior year, so was I. He played basketball and is fiercely competitive, as I was competitive on the swim team. His biological father loves to cook and once opened a café. David went to a culinary school and cooks for many events. He and my two sons both love to climb mountains, camp and fish. What fun memories my sons would have experienced, if they'd had the chance.

I squirmed inside learning about his way of life and tried in vain to reconstruct it; I wanted him to switch gears and become a California guy. He is the product of the family who raised him. David has a strong sense of self-worth of who he is and relishes his country roots. He would have been 10–12 years old before I was mature enough to be a good and responsible mother. No matter how deeply I love him, I was too young to have a baby and raise him. But if I had been given the chance, I am sure I could have pulled it off. Maybe he would have married and raised his children. Or perhaps he would have run away from home and settled in Arkansas. This question has no answer. He's a grown man and there are no retakes.

Recently my niece Tammy and I flew to Arkansas for a visit. We went to dinner and Cajun food on the Arkansas River. We held our stomachs and pleaded for David to stop; our stomachs hurt from laughing. He never stopped. He was on a roll as he sat in his chair shooting off one-liners with an exaggerated accent.

David took us to his parents' deteriorating farm house. There, we found a box, and in it was the baby book I had so long ago handed over to the new parents. David had never seen the book. Together we opened it, only to discover that my head had been cut off in each photo. I screamed and he laughed. I let out a lifetime of anger and he continued to ad lib and smooth my temper. Tammy stepped back. I took the baby book, David found his long lost belt buckle and Tammy took a pendant printed—Booger Holler.

I found my little baby son, and every day when I wake up I know where all of my kids are, and this soothes a mother's soul.

EPILOGUE

WHERE ARE THEY NOW?

JUDI

I am a business owner, a wife and mother and a grandmother. There is a point in life when you need to reflect; this is my time. A birth mother who doesn't have a support system will carry this stigma and burden of relinquishment to her grave. The process of finding my son and letting go of the fantasy of raising him was painful. My grown son is true to himself and his upbringing. I accept him and love him for who he is, not who I expected him to be.

We moved to Lakeport my senior year, and I was happy. All of my friends in Porterville were a year ahead of me and off to college, so it didn't matter if I left. My father did what he thought was the best solution to begin a new life. I met Linda; we sailed every day after school. I met Elaine who was as silly as Trudy and as sweet as Joanie. I went steady for a year with a boy named, oddly enough, Tom. This time, our relationship was pure and innocent. He's kept my secret until this day. I made lots of new lifelong friends. Our graduating class of 42 kids was the perfect place to find myself. I cherish my days in Lakeport. I also gained a step brother, George. He is four years older than me and we are as close as natural siblings.

My step mother was not like anyone I had ever met. She was flamboyant, brilliant, sexy, and she loved her vodka Collins. I am a better person from having her in my life, but it was a difficult journey as I felt a strong attachment to my mother, and didn't want to cheat on her.

True to textbook studies, my life has been beating with a wounded heart as I tried to rejoin the mainstream. The book *Musings of a Ghost Mother* by Lynne Reyman, Ph.D. explains that the pattern of a birth mother is to marry and become a mother as soon as possible to replace her child. I married young at 21, birthed a son Jeff, and left this marriage after four years for unclear reasons, although clear to me now.

Soon after, I remarried and birthed two more children, Dana and Spencer. I began the rewarding role of mom and housewife. Sadly, this marriage lasted only twelve years; we divorced and I left him in search of peace. We tried to make the pieces of the puzzle fit, but they never did. He and I could have made our marriage work with the aid of counseling, but we were both impatient. One year later I began a lengthy relationship and the healing process began. My boyfriend was a positive influence on my children, and I gained confidence. Seven years passed, then we went our separate ways. Seven months later I met my husband, Pete.

When Pete and I met it was an instant connection. He held the key that unlocked my cell of self destruction. He gave me space and released my insecure demons. He let me grieve and encouraged me to do whatever was in my heart. I began to trust a man's judgment and feel safe and on solid ground. We have been married for 16 years and are going strong.

I raised three children to adulthood: Jeff, Dana and Spencer. Our home was full of life, bicycles, outside play, forts, birthday parties and warmth. We had a swimming pool, lots of yelling Marco Polo, family dinners and vacations.

Unprepared, we faced the unimaginable. Jeff passed away in September, soon after his twenty-first birthday. Jeff's sudden death bonded me and my two youngest children even tighter, as we coped with our loss. I fell into a depression, but out of necessity continued to work as a hairdresser. A friend tutored my two children in their studies. We stuck close together and day by day we began to heal and cope.

My children grew to be secure, high functioning adults with loving natures and good choices in life. I met Pete when Dana was 19 and Spencer was 17. Pete and I co-parented his two children on a part-time basis, Kari who was 12 and Alex who was 5 when we met.

I've been a hairdresser since 1965. I have owned three salons and am a past color educator for L'Oreal. My third salon, Satori Color and Hair Design, is in partnership with my daughter Dana who is at the helm while I scale down on my work days and run the salon from behind the scenes. Spencer, my youngest son, married Cassie who is in the last year of her PhD program at UNR in Nevada. Spencer is a Math and Science middle school teacher. Dana and Bill have two daughters, Audrey and Gemma. Kari and Dale have three boys, Gavin, Sawyer and Hudson. Alex will graduate from Chico State University in spring of 2011. I have grandchildren in Arkansas from David: Haley attends Arkansas Tech, Payton is a senior, Jonathon works in Little Rock, Vanessa lives in New Mexico. Being a grandmother is a role I cherish and savor. I have resorted to shameless dress-up games, cupcake makings, flashlights and hiding places, art projects and chase.

My friendships continue with everyone mentioned in this book.

My mother lives close by and resides in a rest home. She is 91. I'm her conservator and keep a close eye on her. Mother is in a wheelchair and I push her for long walks to see the sights or look for husband material. I put my face into hers and tell her my name and family news. She smiles and picks up my hand and kisses it. These are the times I keep close to my heart.

I legally changed my last name to Loren, my father's middle name. This keeps his memory alive and with me.

The secret to life is to be honest with yourself and find your path. The tapestry you've made from life's choices is who you are. Cherish your design.

I've lost two sons, one to adoption, the other in death. There are many avenues to cope and heal. For me, the initial healing process was three-fold: find my son, locate Beth, and confront my past. Later on in life

it was to grieve and deal with Jeff's death and to write my story.
I hope every birth mother or adoptee will use my story to heal your heart, begin your search, and forgive your parents or whomever you blame. Open your eyes; it's okay.

   —Judi Loren Grace

BETH

Thirty-five years passed when an insatiable urge came over me; I had to find my roommate and friend. I exhausted my search on the computer. Weeks passed, months passed, then one weekend I remembered her senior picture. I'd tucked it away for safe keeping. I rushed outside to the garage to take a look inside my steamer trunk.

I set aside a large bag of potting soil, removed a heap of cleaning towels, and removed lumber for a project long overdue. The lid came up with a screech and my life unfolded. I removed Dana's prom dress, my children's art projects, Spencer's teddy bear and Jeff's knit sweater, a baseball mitt, a boy scout shirt and a Blue Bird dress, some yellowed newspapers and my grandmothers quilt; then I saw the box. On the bottom of the trunk sat a flat orange vinyl box I had saved for special things. I put the lid down on the trunk and sat on it, then gently lifted the orange lid. I sorted through letters long forgotten, looked at my mother's church hankie, removed papers and poems. Then I saw her face; it's Beth's senior picture. I flipped it over and there was her parent's address. Shaking at the prospect of being so close, I reminded myself, time has passed and the chances are slim. It was 1997.

I sent a letter to the address she'd written on the back of the photo. This letter is generic as I have no idea who will be on the receiving end. I left my business phone as the contact number. Two weeks passed; I was cutting hair when the salon phone went to message. A deep sexy voice came on the speaker and she says, "I hear you are looking for me. This is Beth." I did a sprint across the floor and grabbed the receiver and yelled her name. Her voice raised a few octaves and she squealed, "Judi?" We giggled and talked at the same time. Later I called her back when I had a break from work; it was magical. We recharged our memories and exchanged stories while in our time warp.

My daughter was living in Europe at the time of our connection. Beth and I celebrated our reunion by flying to London for two weeks. She surprised me with a limo ride to the San Francisco airport. She popped the champagne; we clicked our glasses and said, "Here's to us." We stood in front of the Tower of London and had our picture taken and wrote across the bottom: The Home. Dana took us on many excursions, castles, churches, and local eateries.

We were at ease with each other and relaxed in our room after the long flight. Nothing had changed between us; time stood still. We were finally able to share our birthing stories. Dr. Copeland delivered both our babies and Mrs. Black was our nurse.

She told me that directly after giving birth she kept with her plan and put her baby up for adoption. Her baby left with the social worker and Beth left out the back door alone. The two week waiver grew closer; Beth suffered and had a mini breakdown. She phoned social services and retrieved her daughter.

She brought her baby home to her parents' house where she lived. Beth made a baby bed by adding soft blankets inside of her bottom dresser drawer. She sat next to her baby and waited. Beth relived her story; she heard her dad walk through the front door after work; he walked past her bedroom door, looked in and stopped dead in his tracks and asked, "Why is there a baby in your drawer?"

Well guess what, she didn't go to secretarial school after all.

Beth named her daughter LaNiece.

Beth married, and gave birth to her second child, a son, Mercer. Her children are beautiful and smart, both college graduates, both with successful careers. Just like their mom, her kids have style and class.

Beth is single now by choice and happy; she still calls the shots. She's a successful business woman, which comes as no surprise.

She still has the bunny cookie jar.

FATHER
My father lived to be 74; his death was tragic and accidental.

He and my mother reconciled after the adoption of my son was complete. Seven months later, in June after my junior year, we moved to Lakeport, 400 miles north. He was hired by the County as the Agriculture Commissioner in 1963.

He met Marion who was on the hiring board. My mother moved back to our hometown after six months, and I stayed with my father my senior year. We enjoyed living in a quaint town nestled on the shores of Clear Lake.

A few months after my mother left, my father rented a room above a store to be close to Marion's work. I lived alone my senior year. They married two months after my high school graduation in 1964.
Marion and my father lived in the same home where she and her three siblings had been born and raised. She was the first Miss Lake County. Their home glistened with gold wallpaper and chandeliers and memories.

She changed my father's name from Charlie to Chuck and he happily answered to this. We both had taken new identities, he with a new name, me with a secret tucked deep inside. He flourished in his new marriage: gourmet meals, flaming desserts, pancakes in shapes of Mickey Mouse, intricate landscapes. He also sang in a barber shop quartet.

He was voted Man of the Year; he and Marion were Grand Marshalls in the 4th of July parade. He blossomed with new interests, a new wife, and they achieved a higher status in the community. He planted hundreds of pines along Highway 20. Highway beautification was a project introduced by Lady Bird Johnson; he received a letter of congratulations from her.

My father enjoyed retirement, played the piano, took up painting and decorating Christmas ornaments. He was loved by all who knew him. He memorized one joke after another. Although consumed with telling jokes and stories, he was weak in the deep conversation department.

When I found my son, in 1984 my father paid for David's airfare. We celebrated with family in their backyard in Lakeport. My father took David aside and asked him to please forgive him; he took full blame and responsibility for the adoption. He told David he would be honored if he called him Grandpa.

He retired from Agriculture Commissioner in 1982. He enjoyed fishing, family and fables. His life was perfect.

One Saturday morning, in 1990, I kidnapped him along with my two youngest children, Dana and Spencer. Jeff chose to stay home. We drove him to the Pacific Coast for the day. He became our tour guide and told us about the trees, shrubs, ponds, wild life and Indian history. A treasured road trip, laughing and learning as we headed to the ocean town of Fort Bragg.

Three months after our road trip, my father died from an accidential shooting. He was in ICU for six weeks. Spencer relayed his last visit to me. He said grandpa began to sing to him. He sang to his youngest grandson until he was too weak, but continued until he could only mouth the words. My father loved his grandchildren and he left behind fond memories. His untimely death is difficult to comprehend to this day.

MOTHER

Life has not been easy for my sweet, gentle mother. She suffered a stroke when I was 3, Bobbie 9. The second stroke occurred when I was fifteen, soon after my return home from having my baby. The divorce was difficult for her. Then they reconciled, and life seemed to be heading in a positive direction.

My father falling in love with Marion was a crucial blow. Mother moved back to our hometown and continued through life, attending church and staying close to her mother and her sister. Her home was always open to family and friends. It amazed me that she could whip up a meal for anyone who dropped in unexpectedly. This is a gift I've not yet mastered.

I moved home soon after my high school graduation in 1964. Mother welcomed me with open arms. We shared a double bed and I commuted to Visalia to attend Beauty College. Mother washed and ironed my only uniform and off I'd go the next day. We enjoyed a close bond and I cherish this time in our lives. We ate together, slept together, watched shows on television. Bobbie stopped by with her kids and my friends came over; food and laughter filled our small home.

Bobbie and I watched as Mother's physical health continued to deteriorate. Mother seemed lost and sad. Grandma worried about her daughter's health and mental state and asked me to keep a close eye on her. I tried not to mention my father or his new life in Lakeport.

One day mother was going door to door delivering flyers, an invitation from her church. She met a man who, as he says, was on his knees praying for someone to come into his life. Knock, knock, knock. They ran away two weeks later and married. Floyd was a bona fide nut. He loved my mother dearly and took good care of her, but he was not on the same playing field as most people. She and Floyd were married seven years, until his death from cancer in 1977.

Mother moved to the Pacific coast to be close to Bobbie. I had more time to care for her, since Bobbie worked full time, so Jeff and I moved her back with us to northern California. I had three kids and a mother to keep a close eye on. Mother helped fold clothes and do the dishes. She cut up vegetables for dinner, or sat with the children and showed them how to darn socks. Sometimes the kids played on her walker and tossed blankets over it to make a fort.

Years passed and I became her conservator. Mother resides in a nursing facility. She is gentle and sweet and tells all the nurses thank you. Her oldest granddaughter, Tammy, keeps a close eye on her grandmother whom she affectionately refers to as Nanny.

Jeff was born on his grandma's 50th birthday. Every year we celebrated as a duo party. When Jeff died, I went to the rest home, sat on the edge of her bed, and told her the tragic news; we cried and held each other. She was there with me; she understood.

She has dementia, and lately she is experiencing seizures. She still asks about my father and she knows about Jeff's passing. She remembers the baby I had when I was young. Some events never leave our memory.

RITA, MURRAY, DENNIS AND TRUDY

Rita was 26 years old with a bright future in computers. She commuted to Fresno from a small town east toward the hills. On her way to work one day in her newly painted golden Austin Healy, she was run off the road. A man on a tractor witnessed this careless act by three men. Her car spun out of control and flipped her onto the thousands of boulders that dot the landscape. Rita was in a coma for three months and suffered short-term memory loss for the rest of her life, along with many ailments due to multiple broken bones.

Murray and I visited her in Eugene, Oregon where she lived with her mother who cared for her. Once Rita drove to my front door using cue cards, a seven-hour drive.

Rita lived to be 62. She died due to respiratory problems. She phoned me two days before her death; I had no idea the doctors had told her she had only days to live. Maybe she forgot. I'm told by her caretaker that she requested a root beer float, but the doctors refused her request. That evening Rita got into a wheelchair, took the elevator to the main floor to the cafeteria, ordered a root beer float, charged it to her room, enjoyed her treat, then wheeled back upstairs, got back into bed and passed away two days later. She was a fighter and a free thinker all the way to the end.

Judy Murray went on to be a hotshot model in San Francisco. Married for ten years, she divorced and moved south of the Bay Area where she found her passion. She is a house painter, a reader, a collector. She is elusive and funny. Unfortunately we don't see each other for years at a time, but when we do get together, we meet with Dennis and eat and laugh as if no time has passed. She is as cool as they come.

Dennis stands tall at 6'6" he is a retired high school teacher and career counselor. He lives in a beautiful home on Scenic Heights overlooking our hometown. I always stay at his house when I visit. He is a magical cook, specializing in Mexican dishes. Dennis was my first date; I asked him to the King's Fling. After the dance when he took me home, we sat on the front porch and ate Fritos and Eskimo Pies with my mother.

Trudy lives on the Pacific coast and owns Ostrichland. Her store and land were used in the movie *Sideways*. She is semi-divorced, busy and happy. Trudy is a talented artist and presents herself as a cute giggly blond, but she is an astute and successful business woman, make no mistake about that. Trudy maintains her youthful appearance and is as peppy as always. Just like us, our parents were best friends in high school. When I think of my childhood, I think of Trudy. She was also one of my friends who drove to Exeter with a baby gift .

MIKE

I didn't see Mike for 10 years. I was in my hometown for the once-a-year big event Veterans Day Parade and Celebration and for a weekend with old friends. I ran into him while out. He apologized, invited me to go to an *Up with Jesus* concert, and I went. He brought me a Bible the next day. He apologized again for his bad judgment call in the spring of '62. He told me he mailed his friend Tom a father's day card each year for many years.

Mike is married and has three children. He eventually zeroed in on his passion and became a well-known rodeo clown. He traveled most of the United States and found his fame and joy. He was also a chaplain and prayed with groups of cowboys before each rodeo.

He ultimately became a police officer and retired as a rodeo clown after many head-on collisions with bulls. He resides with his wife Davalynn in Colorado and remains a good and loyal friend.

JOANIE

Joanie married Bill in 1964. They raised three children and, in the midst of being a wife and mother, she managed to go back to school and receive her teaching credential. Joanie was an elementary school teacher until her retirement in 2005. Her grandson Beau was in one of her classes. She has never changed; she is soft spoken, shy and knows who she is. Her loyalty never wavers. She continues to be involved with the theater and she volunteers at the local museum.

She and Bill recently celebrated 46 years of marriage. Bill is the high school music teacher. They live alone with their little dachshund Wolfie, whom she lovingly refers to as her little ankle biter. They live 35 miles from where we grew up.

Joanie kept every one of the letters I diligently sent her from my hiding place in Oakland. She gingerly handed them over and I had to swear on a stack of Bibles to keep them safe and return them promptly. The letters are a great resource and a treasure. *(See Letters to Joanie.)* I not only wrote to her about daily life in the Home, but drew diagrams of each floor with room numbers and locations. I was able to reconstruct the inside of the Home to bring you my story.

I really did receive a letter from Joanie one hour prior to my delivery.

She remains my close and trusted friend.

BOBBIE

My sister Bobbie married Jerry, the love of her life. She and her husband chose State jobs working in mental hospitals in Porterville and Atascadero, both locked facilities. Each took early retirement while in their 50s.

We are not as close as we once were. Bobbie and I have different interests and lifestyles, but when we do get together, we laugh easily and talk about our family, our past. Bobbie lives a quiet, serene life in Northern California.

She has battled cancer twice. She is a fighter; she's tough and blessed. One would never guess she has suffered such intense pain. Jerry takes good care of her when needed.

Bobbie and Jerry are involved in church, and she plays cards with her women friends once a week. She loves to cook for large crowds and she still sews, but not maternity smocks. She is happy and content with her life and marriage. They live quietly with their huge brown dog Woody, who is afraid of the dark and noises.

Bobbie has two grown children, Tammy and Roger and four grandchildren. Her blended family also includes Jerry's three adult daughters and their children.

Sometimes I still see her as my young, dark-haired sister who helped me, sewed for me, and offered me her gold ring for the summer.

Uncle Bill

Uncle Bill worked up the ladder of success as the Agriculture Commissioner, residing in our State capitol, Sacramento. My father, his friend, helped him get his start in this field. His kids are grown and he and my Aunt Doris were living the good life. At age 52 he went for his usual morning jog, returned home, sat down to read the paper and suffered a massive heart attack. His funeral was huge; he was loved by many. No one wailed louder than me.

The year of his passing was 1971, only nine years since his visit and his gift of the box of chocolates. He left his son Jack and daughter Sharon. Soon after his death, Sharon had her third baby boy and named him William.

REVISITING THE HOME

Once again David flew in to Sacramento; we planned a weekend of adventure. The drive to San Francisco was entertaining with Spencer and David in the car. We had lunch at Pier 39, then hopped a ferry to Alcatraz for a tour. After the ferry delivered us back to the pier, we drove to Oakland to meet Beth and confront the past.

Beth's living room was ablaze with conversation with my two sons and her daughter. We talked about London and our excursions. The boys visited with Beth, but her daughter was stand-offish. She wasn't sure of our relationship, who we were. Beth had never told her daughter about living in the Home; her daughter thought she was born at Kaiser. She asked her mom why she didn't tell her, and true to form, Beth answered back, "You never asked."

Beth has never driven by the Home, even though she lives a few miles away. Beth said she couldn't go back. I suggested we go there for closure.

In a caravan with Beth and I in the lead, we drove toward the looming stone monster. Beth drove us, said she was feeling nervous. I confessed my palms were sweaty, and I had a knot in my stomach. She turned onto Garden Street. We were a mess, but we needed to face our past. Three cars pulled to the curb. We saw the wide concrete steps and the same wrought iron hand rail. We got out, David ran ahead of us to the top of the steps, stopped and said, "I was born in a parking lot?" The building had sat high above the street; we didn't realize until that moment it was gone, flattened by the quake in 1989. The landscape is still there and looks the same. I felt let down, but also set free.

The five of us walked on the debris where a building once stood. Beth and I stood together in one particular spot, with our feet planted firmly on the ground. We showed the kids where our bedroom was located, next to the Chinese elm that still stood tall and swayed in the breeze above us. We walked to where the dining room had been, the laundry room, the delivery room; we kicked at the dirt and weeds. We both noticed something on the ground. There were a few tiny white octagonal tiles lying in the dirt, the same tiles that lined the shower in the labor room. I picked one up and David picked one up and listened to us as we recreated the surroundings. Then her daughter found one and so did Spencer. We each kept the worn, dull, white tile as a symbol. We walked to the driveway and showed our kids where we used to play hopscotch. The crafts store was still there too. I stood with Beth and told her that after she went upstairs to have her baby I was depressed and walked away from the Home and walked until I got to the Sears store. She told me I had walked 10 miles that day.

I walked down the driveway with my tall sons on either side, the same driveway my sister and mother had driven up to retrieve me and my baby, the same driveway all of our friends had made their exit, with or without their babies. At the end of the driveway stood the same sign: "One Way Out." Beth took a picture of me and David standing by the sign. I needed closure, and she needed to come clean with her daughter Niecee.

Our caravan drove to Berkeley; we ate fish and chips. We toasted and laughed and shared stories. Spencer had one story after another and was our comic relief. After our dinner, we went outside and prepared for the long ride home. Everyone hugged, lingering over conversations and good-byes. David was touched. When he climbed into the car, he said Beth's daughter Niecee gave him a big hug and said, "Nice meeting you, roommate."

Dad

Dad Centennial Beard Contest

Judi, Dad and Bobbie

1964 Lakeport Teens

The Porterville Orange Blossoms

The Porterville Fair

Centennial Girls Judy, Judi, and Andrea

Mom

Dad at Centennial Celebration

Mom

Judi Archery Classs

Bobbie

Judi Dancing

Bobbie

Joanie and Murray

Rodeo Clown Mike

Joanie and Judi

Bill and Joanie

Judi

Rita

Murray

Dennis

Trudy

Judi in Rita's Austin Healy

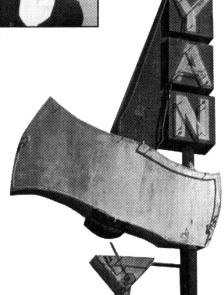

188

Beth's Senior Photo

Judi's Senior Photo

Beth and Judi at site of Home

Beth and Judi

Niecee and Beth's sister

Judi and David

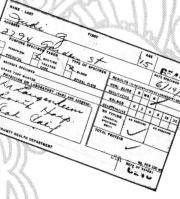

David, Judi, Jeff, Spencer, and Dana

Alex, Pete, Judi, Spencer, and Dana

Judi, Dad and Bobbie

Kari, Spencer, Dana and Alex

Mom and Judi

Judi and Jeff

Judi and Tammy

Pete and Judi

David

Yesterday I had
precious correspondent, July 6
Well I received your letter on a Friday
get around to answering it until
morning on a Friday.
You sound very wrapped up in
2794 Garden St.
Oakland, California
OAKLAND
1962
CALIF.
2794 Garden St.
Oakland 1, California
JOANIE
1389 K
Porterv

LETTERS TO JOANIE

June 23, 1962
Dear Joanie,
I forgot to tell you, when you address my letter put Judi G. and that's all.
You have to put the G. but don't spell it out.

I hope you don't think I get homesick after the first couple of days away from
home, but under these circumstances, up here and everything; with 50 girls
believe me love, it can become pretty depressing.
My pad number is
Judi G.
P.O. Box 7023 Fruitvale Station
Oakland, California.

P.S. every time I send you a letter, I'll send you a ball off my bedspread, o.k.?
Then when I get home, you can make me another bedspread.

If you send me 70 cents I can make you a pair of slippers in 2 days. If you
do, what color do you want? Purple, red, blue, or black?? Or mixed, I'll
surprise you.
Love Judi

July 17, 1962
Dear Joanie,
Don't get the idea that I'm having one big blast cause honey I'm not. I miss everyone & every little thing about my home. So much I almost cry at night I get so depressed, but I hold it back, after all, I have another 2 months to go.... boo hoo!!

I hope we are still as close as we were. I'm afraid we won't have anything in common. Don't get too lonesome, at least you've got your family with you. So perk up and quit feeling sorry for yourself. Try being me. Ha ha; just kidding.

Oh damn that Tom. If only I had stayed with Dewain, we could still be going on picnics and acting like big goofs. But thanks to my simple mind our friendship will probably never be the same. I wish I hadn't slapped him so many times. I guess I slapped the wrong guy. I hope you still want to confide in me in the future. I doubt if I'll have much to confide to you.
I'm glad you miss me, I'm not very mushy as you know, but in my stone heart I miss you too. I took my measurements last night. I'm 38-33-39, pretty curvy huh. I doubt if I will ever be able to wear your copper belt again, not ever. For the past two nights about 12 girls have met in the parlor and we dance. I've learned to do the Continental walk, Texas Hop, Watusi and the Bristol Stomp.

I started doing exercises. I do 60 touch toes so my muscles will go back into shape quicker and 30 squats so I'll have an easier delivery (I hope).
God, how did this happen. I want to come home so badly, but I would die if anyone saw me. Thank you so much for being my friend and not leaving me. I'll be looking at the moon, but I'll be seeing you.

Sept. 1 MY MONTH

Hi Joanie, You sound like you had one big blast up in long Beach. Do you have a real good tan? I'm trying my best to keep up with you.

We start school here Sept. 4th. How does it feel to be a big senior? Those poor underclassmen are so immature!

Oh, let me tell you. Last night a girl had her baby, she was the fifth one in the last two days, but she was in labor for 24 hours and 15 min. I went up to the third floor to get some medicine and that poor girl was in the labor room crying, then she would moan, and yell, oh, you can't imagine, the first one I have ever heard. It shook me up. By the way, the doctor, the colored man, (he's real nice, I like him a lot) looked at my toe and it is healing, then he told me I have very high arches and pretty feet. So you can touch one when I come home in about 3 weeks.

P.S. The smell of my last letter is "French Lace." Do you like it?

September 12

Dear Joanie, I can't lie on my left side cause the head or something is way over to one side. I can't lay on my stomach cause I get sick, so when I get back home I'll probably have a flat head from lying on my back. I wish I could talk to you. I'm scared to death of labor. The girls all look like monsters when they come out of the delivery room. 3 nights ago, I grabbed a leg and I could actually feel its feet.

Well, it's another day (the next morning) and I feel better, I'm not so depressed today.

Bye Judi

It will probably be better for me to go to school in Visalia when I come home-the kids in P'ville will treat me like dirt for the rest of my life and I couldn't take that.

I'm really surprised we've kept in touch ALL summer. But I'm glad we did. In your last letter you said you hope we see each other again. Honey, don't ever forget this, as long as I have my Opel and they sell Flying A gas I can drive up any ol' time. O.K.?? Hey, they called clinic—here goes again. Well, I finally got out of clinic. He played around on my stomach for a long time then said, "You're doing very well." Then he took "its" heart beat, and then he took my hands and put them down on the sides and he moved my hands around and Joanie, I'm not kidding, I actually felt its head. Wooooo- was it ever exciting.
Well that's about all for now. Bye Judi

September 19th Wednesday
Hi Joanie,
Sorry I haven't written but you know how it is when you have a baby!! Yes, aren't you proud of me?

I delivered at 2:08 Monday afternoon. I went into labor about 9:00 p.m. Friday night. It was an awfully long labor but it was worth every minute, (I'll tell you all the details when I get home.) I'm leaving here Monday the 24th.
I had a boy, Mom and Bobbie decided on Robert Charles for the name. He weights 7 lbs 12 oz (big huh) 20 inches long and he has reddish hair.

Since the baby was so big, I have stitches to my rectum and that's a lot of stitches. In fact, this is more painful than labor. No, I take that back.
Well, I best close, my stitches are smarting.
Just think, I'll be home soon. I miss our talks in the park and our next one should be a dilly.
Love ya, Judi and Robert

RESOURCES

Below are excerpts from the book *Musings of a Ghost Mother* by Lynne Reyman (Oroville, CA, I & L Publishing, 2001). This is a book which documents the chronic, long-lasting grief of women who relinquished infants for adoption in the 1950s and 60s. Secret stuff has a way of oozing out. Sometimes secrets explode. Secret keepers in the world of adoption play a dangerous and heartless game.

"Part of what still haunts me as a birth mother is that I was told, and I believed, that I had no value to the daughter that I relinquished. I understood that I was of no consequence to my baby. I could be replaced and forgotten. I was inconsequential. That feeling still lived deep inside of me twenty years later. I feared it might be true." (Reyman, p. 47)

"...Whether or not the mother will attempt to reunite with her child lost to adoption, her long-term adjustment includes learning to live with the longing. She can never go back and parent her child as an infant, toddler, school-age child, and teenager. On a deeper level, it is a journey of mind, heart and soul which offers the opportunity to reawaken what is already wise and strong within oneself." (Reyman, p. 44)

"Birth mothers were routinely advised that in time the relinquishment would be forgotten and life would resume normally. But as Roles noted, living with the uncertainty of knowing how her child is faring has been identified by birth parents as the most difficult aspect of coping."
Lynne Reyman, Ph.D. quotes P. Roles: *Saying Goodbye to a Baby*
(*The Birth Parent's Guide to Loss and Grief, in Adoption, Vol. 1,*
(Washington, D.C., Child Welfare League of America) (Reyman, p. 40)

"*In the heyday of relinquishment, of course, the birth mother's usefulness was complete once she had delivered a healthy baby.*" Lynne Reyman, Ph.D.

This is a quote from the daughter Lynne Reyman relinquished at birth and subsequently found after a lengthy search:
"*After giving the baby up, she stopped laughing. The kind of laugh that comes from the inside was gone ... When she started to search out the adult child, she started looking for that laugh again. Looking for the part of her that got left behind.*" (Reyman, p. 39)

"*On the other hand, some birth mothers find it difficult to attach to subsequent children. As noted previously, a high percentage of birth mothers never have another child, often out of guilt, a sense that it would be a betrayal to the child she let go.*" (Reyman, p. 39)

"*Of course, if a birth mother grew up in a family with secrets and closed communication she is already conditioned to develop and maintain a false self: the pretense is as natural as breathing. Just a few more common triggers include invitations to baby showers, the sight of other mother's get-togethers with their babies (even after birthing subsequent children), the anniversary of the lost child's birthday, songs that were popular at the time of pregnancy and relinquishment, the innocent and the deadly question 'How many children do you have?'*" (Reyman, p. 27)

Patricia E. Tayor gets it exactly right when she says, *"The most important thing to remember about 1961 was firmly embedded in the rules, mores and values of the fifties and before. Women were allowed to further their education, but their ultimate goal was to achieve the title of 'Mrs.' Men were to work to support their families: women stayed home to care of those families. If a woman worked, she was taking that job from a man. Women were not even supposed to call men on the phone. They were expected to sit home and wait to be called. Women who were daring enough to call men were considered aggressive. Women who were 'pregnant too soon' were 'in trouble'. I would add that pregnant girls were expelled from school and pregnant women could be refused employment."* Patricia Taylor, Ph.D., *Shadow Train* (in Reyman, p. 15.)

I was especially consumed with Lynne Reyman's chapter entitled *Triggers*. This is about Post-Traumatic Stress Disorder. It is vital to read this book to understand the long term ramifications of relinquishment and the veil of shame that shrouds us, such as early marriages ending in divorce after a child is conceived, or leaving one relationship after another. Not all, but a very high percentage of birthmothers are looking for the perfect fit, or the relationship that will bring the young mother contentment.
—Judi Loren Grace